London for Families

Explore Top Attractions, Parks, and Fun Activities with Kids

Lowell Gore

All rights reserved. No part of this publication may be reproduced, distributed, or transmitted in any form or any means, including photocopying, recording, or other electronic or mechanical methods, without the prior written permission of the publisher, except in the case of brief quotations embodied in critical reviews and certain other noncommercial uses permitted by copyright law.
Copyright © (Lowell Gore)

Table of contents

Introduction:.................................... 6

Welcome to London
Why London for Families

Planning Your Trip:........................ 13

Best Times to Visit
Budgeting for a Family Trip
Travel Insurance and Safety Tips
Essential Packing List

Getting to London:........................ 35

Major Airports
How to Get to the City
Train and Bus Options
Navigating London with Kids

Accommodation: 48
Family-Friendly Hotels
Apartments and Vacation Rentals
Unique Stays
Tips for Finding the Best Deals

Getting Around London: 75
Public Transport
Walking and Biking
Family-Friendly Options

Top Attractions for Families: 96
Historical Sites
Museums
Parks and Outdoor Spaces
Entertainment

Day Trips from London: 124
Harry Potter Studio Tour
Windsor Castle
Legoland Windsor
Brighton Beach

Eating Out with Kids: 148

Family-Friendly Restaurants
Cafes and Bakeries
Picnicking Spots
Special Dietary Needs

Fun and Free Activities: 177

Free Museums and Galleries
Parks and Playgrounds
Walking Tours
Seasonal Events and Festivals

Shopping with Kids: 188

Toy Stores and Bookshops
Markets and Malls
Souvenirs and Keepsakes

Cultural Tips and Etiquette: 196

Understanding British Manners
Navigating Cultural Differences
Tips for a Smooth Stay

Health and Safety: 204

Nearest Hospitals and Clinics
Emergency Numbers
Child Safety Tips

Tips for an Unforgettable Trip: 212

Creating an Itinerary
Keeping Kids Entertained
Making the Most of Your Visit

Useful Resources: 220

Apps for Navigating London

Maps: 224

Introduction

Welcome to London

Welcome to London, a city where the past and present blend seamlessly. As you arrive in this lively metropolis, you'll be met with iconic landmarks, top-notch attractions, and a rich cultural scene that promises an unforgettable experience for you and your family.

London is full of stories. Imagine standing on the ancient streets of the Tower of London, thinking about the tales of kings, queens, knights, and prisoners that have played out within its walls.

The Yeoman Warders, or Beefeaters, will entertain you with captivating and often amusing stories that make history come alive in a way that books can't match.

One of my best memories is seeing my kids' eyes widen in awe as they looked at the Crown Jewels. They were amazed by the glittering crowns and scepters, and they couldn't stop talking about them long after we left.

Before you start your London adventure, here are a few helpful tips to make getting around easier.

Get There Early: Famous spots like the Tower of London and Buckingham Palace can get busy. Arriving early not only helps you avoid the crowds but also lets you enjoy a quieter experience.

Use Public Transport: London's public transport system is efficient and family-friendly. The Underground, buses, and even riverboats make exploring the city simple. An Oyster card is handy for easy travel.

Dress for the Weather: London's weather can be unpredictable. Wear layers and always carry an umbrella, just in case it rains.

Traveling with family is all about creating memories that will last a lifetime. London offers countless chances for such moments.

From watching the Changing of the Guard at Buckingham Palace to riding the London Eye and seeing panoramic views of the city, each experience is a piece of a wonderful memory.

So, whether you're here for a short visit or a longer stay, London is ready to welcome you with open arms.

It's a city where every corner has a story, and each visit promises new adventures.

I hope this guide helps you discover the charm of London, and that you and your family leave with hearts full of joy and lots of great stories to share.

Why London is Perfect for Families

London is a city that offers endless opportunities for families to explore, learn, and have fun together. Here's why I believe London is the perfect destination for families, based on my own experiences and observations.

A Rich Tapestry of History and Culture

One of the most captivating aspects of London is its rich history and diverse culture. Walking through the city, you'll find yourself surrounded by historical landmarks that tell the story of Britain's past.

For instance, the Tower of London is not just a fortress but a place where kids can learn about kings, queens, and even the notorious ravens that guard the grounds.

Insider Tip: Take a guided tour with a Beefeater. These knowledgeable guides bring history to life with fascinating stories and a touch of humor that kids will love.

Museums and Galleries Galore

London is home to some of the world's best museums and galleries, many of which are incredibly family-friendly. The Natural History Museum, with its gigantic dinosaur skeletons and interactive exhibits, is always a hit with children.

Just a short walk away is the Science Museum, where kids can engage with hands-on displays that make learning fun.

Practical Advice: Most of these museums offer free entry, which is great for budgeting families. Arrive early to avoid the crowds, and don't forget to check out the special family activities and workshops often held during school holidays.

Beautiful Parks and Open Spaces

London boasts numerous parks and green spaces perfect for family outings. Hyde Park, for example, offers a range of activities from boating on the Serpentine Lake to visiting the Diana Memorial Playground, inspired by the adventures of Peter Pan.

Regent's Park is another gem, with beautiful gardens, open-air theater performances, and the famous London Zoo.

Storytelling Moment: I remember taking a leisurely boat ride on the Serpentine with my kids. We laughed as we tried to steer and ended up in circles more than once. It's these little moments of joy that make family travel so special.

Easy and Fun Transportation

Getting around London is a breeze thanks to its excellent public transport system. Kids usually find the Tube exciting, especially when you pass through the older, more intricate stations.

Buses are also a great way to see the city from above ground, and a boat trip on the Thames can offer a unique perspective on London's landmarks.

Practical Tips: Get an Oyster card for convenient and affordable travel. Plan your routes in advance, especially if you're traveling with young children, to ensure a smooth journey.

Entertainment for All Ages

London is bursting with entertainment options for families. The West End theater district offers a range of family-friendly shows, from classic musicals to contemporary plays.

Additionally, attractions like the London Eye provide breathtaking views of the city, which are sure to leave both kids and adults in awe.

Engaging Format: Create a checklist of must-see shows and attractions. This not only keeps everyone excited but also helps in planning your itinerary.

Delicious and Diverse Food Options

Eating out in London is an adventure in itself. The city's diverse culinary scene means you can find something to suit every palate. From traditional fish and chips to exotic dishes from around the world, the food options are endless.

Personal Touch: One of our favorite spots is Borough Market, where we can sample a variety of foods and the kids love the bustling atmosphere. Watching their faces light up as they try new flavors is always a delight.

Safe and Welcoming Environment

London is known for being a safe and welcoming city. The locals are generally friendly and helpful, and there are plenty of resources available for families.

Whether it's child-friendly facilities in public places or family-focused events and activities, London ensures that families feel comfortable and well-cared for.

Final Tips: Always keep an eye on your belongings, as you would in any big city. Make use of family rooms in attractions and parks, which are often equipped with everything you might need for a comfortable visit.

Planning Your Trip

Best Times to Visit

Deciding when to visit London can make a big difference in your family's experience. Each season offers unique attractions and activities, so here's a breakdown to help you choose the best time for your trip.

Spring (March to May)

Spring is a wonderful time to visit London. The city comes alive with blooming flowers and milder temperatures, making it perfect for outdoor activities.

Personal Experience: I remember visiting Kew Gardens in April with my family. The sight of cherry blossoms in full bloom was magical, and the kids loved the interactive exhibits at the Children's Garden.

Practical Tips

Weather: Expect temperatures between 11°C (52°F) and 15°C (59°F). Light jackets and layers are ideal.

Events: Enjoy the Chelsea Flower Show in May, where the gardens are filled with stunning displays.

Crowds: Fewer tourists compared to summer, making popular attractions less crowded.

Summer (June to August)

Summer in London is bustling with tourists and filled with festivals and outdoor events. The long daylight hours mean you can pack more into your day.

Insider Tip: Make the most of the free outdoor events, such as concerts in Hyde Park and open-air theater in Regent's Park.

Weather

Warm and Sunny: Temperatures range from 18°C (64°F) to 30°C (86°F). Pack light clothing, sunscreen, and hats.

Family Fun: Take advantage of school holidays by visiting kid-friendly attractions like the London Zoo and theme parks nearby.

Crowds

Expect Crowds: Popular tourist spots will be busy, so plan to arrive early. Consider booking tickets in advance for major attractions to avoid long lines.

Autumn (September to November)

Autumn is another great time to visit, with fewer crowds and a crisp, cool climate. The fall foliage adds a touch of beauty to the city's parks and gardens.

Storytelling Moment: One of my favorite autumn visits was to Greenwich Park. The leaves were turning shades of red and gold, creating a picturesque backdrop for a family picnic.

We also visited the Royal Observatory, where the kids were fascinated by the astronomy exhibits.

Weather

Cool and Comfortable: Temperatures drop to 11°C (52°F) to 18°C (64°F). Pack warm layers and a waterproof jacket.

Events: Don't miss the Bonfire Night celebrations in early November, featuring fireworks and family-friendly activities.

Crowds

Quieter: With schools back in session, attractions are less crowded. It's a great time for a more relaxed visit.

Winter (December to February)

Winter in London can be chilly, but it's also a time when the city transforms into a festive wonderland. From Christmas markets to ice skating rinks, there's plenty to enjoy.

Personal Touch: I fondly remember our family trip to Winter Wonderland in Hyde Park. The kids had a blast on the rides, and we all warmed up with hot chocolate while watching the Christmas lights twinkle.

Weather

Cold and Crisp: Temperatures can range from 2°C (36°F) to 8°C (46°F). Be sure to pack warm clothes, scarves, and gloves.

Festive Spirit: London's holiday season is magical. Visit the Christmas markets, see the lights on Oxford Street, and go ice skating at Somerset House.

Crowds

Busy During Holidays: The city can be crowded around Christmas and New Year's, so plan accordingly. Attractions may have special holiday hours, so check ahead.

Making the Most of Your Visit

No matter when you decide to visit, London has something special to offer. Here are a few final tips to help you make the most of your trip.

Plan Ahead: Check the weather forecast and local event calendars to pack appropriately and make the most of seasonal activities.

Flexibility: Be flexible with your plans. London's weather can be unpredictable, so have indoor activities in mind as backup options.

Local Insights: Take advantage of local knowledge. Ask locals for recommendations on seasonal events and hidden gems that are perfect for families.

Budgeting for a Family Trip

Planning a family trip to London is an exciting adventure, but it's important to budget wisely to make the most of your experience. Here's a detailed guide on how to manage your finances effectively while ensuring a memorable trip for everyone.

Setting a Budget

The first step is to establish a clear budget. Consider all potential expenses, from flights and accommodation to daily spending on food, attractions, and souvenirs.

Personal Experience: When we planned our family trip to London, we sat down together and listed everything we wanted to do and see. This helped us create a realistic budget and prioritize our spending.

Practical Tips

Research Costs: Look up the average costs of flights, hotels, meals, and attractions. Websites like TripAdvisor and Booking.com are great for getting an idea of prices.

Use a Spreadsheet: Track your expenses in a spreadsheet to keep everything organized and ensure you stay within your budget.

Saving on Flights

Flights can be one of the biggest expenses, but with a bit of planning, you can find good deals.

Insider Tip: Book flights well in advance and use comparison websites like Skyscanner or Kayak to find the best prices. Be flexible with your travel dates if possible, as mid-week flights are often cheaper.

Personal Touch: We booked our flights three months ahead and found a great deal by flying mid-week. It saved us a significant amount, which we used for other activities.

Accommodation Choices

Choosing the right accommodation is crucial. London offers a wide range of options, from budget-friendly hotels to vacation rentals.

Storytelling Moment: During our stay, we opted for a family-friendly Airbnb in a central location. It was more affordable than a hotel and gave us the convenience of having a kitchen to prepare some of our meals.

Practical Advice

Consider Location: Staying in central areas might be more expensive, but it can save you money and time on transportation.

Look for Deals: Use websites like Airbnb, Booking.com, or family-friendly hotel chains that offer discounts or special packages.

Managing Daily Expenses

Daily expenses can add up quickly, especially with a family. Here are some tips to keep costs down while still enjoying your trip.

Eating Out

Budget-Friendly Meals: London has plenty of affordable dining options. Check out local markets like Borough Market for delicious, inexpensive food.

Self-Catering: If your accommodation has a kitchen, consider cooking some meals. It's a great way to save money and experience local supermarkets.

Transport

Oyster Card: Invest in an Oyster card for convenient and cheaper travel on public transport.

Walk and Explore: London is a walkable city. Walking not only saves money but also allows you to discover hidden gems.

Attractions

Free Attractions: Many of London's top attractions, like the British Museum and National Gallery, are free. Plan your visit around these.

Discount Passes: Consider buying a London Pass, which offers discounted entry to multiple attractions.

Extra Tips for Budgeting

Souvenirs: Set a limit on how much you'll spend on souvenirs. Local markets and smaller shops often have more affordable options.

Emergency Fund: Always set aside a small emergency fund for unexpected expenses. This ensures peace of mind during your trip.

Engaging Format: Create a checklist of your expected expenses and regularly update it to stay on track. This can include categories like accommodation, food, transportation, attractions, and souvenirs.

Making the Most of Your Budget

Personal Story: One of the best decisions we made was to allocate a portion of our budget for spontaneous experiences. We ended up taking a boat trip on the Thames, which wasn't initially planned but became one of the highlights of our trip.

Final Tips

Plan Ahead: Research and book in advance to get the best deals.

Be Flexible: Allow room in your budget for unexpected activities or expenses.

Involve the Family: Let everyone participate in budgeting. It teaches kids valuable lessons about money management and makes them feel involved in the planning process.

Travel Insurance and Safety Tips

When planning a family trip to London, ensuring your family's safety and well-being is paramount. Travel insurance and a few essential safety tips can give you peace of mind and help you handle any unexpected situations.

Why Travel Insurance is Essential

Travel insurance is like a safety net that protects you against unforeseen events such as medical emergencies, trip cancellations, and lost luggage.

Personal Experience: I remember the relief we felt when our travel insurance covered the cost of an unexpected doctor visit for one of the kids who fell ill during our trip. Without it, we would have faced a hefty medical bill.

Practical Tips

Choose the Right Plan: Look for comprehensive coverage that includes medical emergencies, trip cancellations, lost or delayed baggage, and personal liability.

Read the Fine Print: Ensure you understand what is covered and what is not. Pay attention to policy exclusions and coverage limits.

Compare Policies: Use comparison websites to find the best policy for your needs and budget.

Selecting the Right Travel Insurance

Selecting the right travel insurance can be overwhelming, but here's how to simplify the process.

Insider Tip: Look for family-specific policies that offer coverage for all members, including children, often at a discounted rate.

Personal Touch: We found a policy that included coverage for adventurous activities, which was perfect since we planned to do some outdoor activities like zip-lining and boating.

Checklist for Choosing Insurance

Medical Coverage: Ensure it covers medical expenses, hospital stays, and emergency evacuations.

Trip Cancellation: This should cover non-refundable costs if you need to cancel your trip due to unforeseen circumstances.

Baggage and Personal Belongings: Coverage for lost, stolen, or damaged baggage and personal items.

Travel Delays: Compensation for delays that result in additional expenses like meals and accommodation.

Safety Tips for Your London Trip

While London is generally a safe city, it's always wise to take precautions to ensure your family's safety.

Stay Informed

Local News and Updates: Keep an eye on local news for any travel advisories or important updates.

Emergency Numbers: Familiarize yourself with local emergency numbers. In London, dial 999 for emergencies.

Health and Well-being

Carry a First Aid Kit: Pack a basic first aid kit with essentials like band-aids, antiseptic wipes, and any prescription medications your family needs.

Stay Hydrated: Carry water bottles, especially if you're visiting during the summer.

Personal Safety

Secure Your Belongings: Use a money belt or a secure bag to keep your valuables safe. Avoid carrying large sums of cash.

Be Aware of Your Surroundings: Stay vigilant, especially in crowded areas. Pickpocketing can be an issue in tourist spots.

Navigating the City

Public Transport Safety: Always keep an eye on your belongings when using public transport. Teach kids to stay close and avoid wandering off.

Emergency Meeting Points: Establish a meeting point in case anyone gets separated. This is particularly useful in busy areas like museums or parks.

Preparing for the Unexpected

Despite the best planning, sometimes things go awry. Here's how to handle unexpected situations.

Lost or Stolen Items

Report Immediately: Report any lost or stolen items to the local authorities and your travel insurance provider as soon as possible.

Keep Copies of Important Documents: Make photocopies of passports, insurance policies, and other important documents. Store them separately from the originals.

Medical Emergencies

Know Your Insurance Details: Carry a copy of your travel insurance policy and emergency contact numbers.

Local Hospitals: Research and note down the nearest hospitals or clinics to your accommodation.

Engaging Format: Create a small checklist for emergency contacts and important numbers, including your travel insurance provider, local hospitals, and emergency services.

Final Thoughts on Safety

Personal Story: One night, we had to deal with a minor medical emergency, and having travel insurance made the situation much less stressful. Knowing we were covered allowed us to focus on getting the right care for our child.

Final Tips

Stay Calm: In case of any emergency, stay calm and follow your plan.

Keep Everyone Informed: Make sure all family members know what to do and where to go in case of an emergency.

Travel insurance and these safety tips can help ensure that your family's trip to London is not only enjoyable but also secure.

Essential Packing List

Packing for a family trip to London can seem daunting, but with a well-thought-out list, you can ensure that you have everything you need for a comfortable and enjoyable stay. Here's a detailed guide to help you pack efficiently and effectively.

Clothing Essentials

London's weather can be unpredictable, so it's important to pack versatile clothing that can handle different conditions.

Layers are Key: The weather can change quickly, so having options makes it easier to stay comfortable. Bring a mix of t-shirts, long sleeves, and sweaters or hoodies that can be added or removed as needed.

Waterproof Jacket: A lightweight, waterproof jacket is a must. We learned this the hard way when a sudden rain shower caught us off guard during a day out. Now, we never travel without one.

Comfortable Shoes: Exploring London means a lot of walking. Comfortable, broken-in shoes are essential. Pack a pair of sturdy sneakers for everyday wear and a nicer pair for evenings out.

Personal Experience: On one trip, we walked over 10 miles in a single day! Having the right footwear made all the difference in keeping your feet happy and ready for more adventures.

Health and Hygiene

Keeping everyone healthy and clean during your trip is crucial.

First Aid Kit: Pack a basic first aid kit with band-aids, antiseptic wipes, pain relievers, and any prescription medications. Having these on hand can save you from having to find a pharmacy in a hurry.

Hand Sanitizer and Masks: In crowded places, it's helpful to have hand sanitizer. We also pack a few masks just in case we need them.

Toiletries: Travel-sized toiletries are convenient. Don't forget essentials like toothbrushes, toothpaste, shampoo, conditioner, soap, and any specific items your family needs.

Personal Touch: I always bring a small pack of tissues and wet wipes. They're incredibly handy for quick clean-ups and freshening up on the go.

Gadgets and Gear

Staying connected and capturing memories are important parts of any trip.

Portable Charger: With so many photo opportunities and the need to navigate using our phones, a portable charger is indispensable. We've often found ourselves running low on battery after a full day of sightseeing.

Universal Adapter: London uses Type G electrical outlets. A universal adapter ensures that you can charge your devices without any issues.

Camera: While phone cameras are great, bringing a good camera can help capture higher-quality memories. We always pack our compact camera for those special shots.

Personal Experience: I remember the joy of looking through the photos we took at the Tower of London. Having a good camera made those memories even more vivid.

Travel Documents

Keeping your travel documents organized is important

Passports and Visas: Ensure all passports are valid for at least six months beyond your travel dates. Check if you need a visa and make sure you have it sorted before you leave.

Travel Insurance: Carry a copy of your travel insurance policy and emergency contact numbers. It's comforting to know you're covered in case of any issues.

Personal Story: We keep a folder with all our travel documents, including flight tickets, hotel reservations, and itinerary. It makes it easy to find everything when needed.

Entertainment and Comfort

Keeping everyone entertained, especially during downtime or travel, is key to a smooth trip.

Books and Games: Pack a few books, magazines, or travel games to keep everyone entertained during flights or train rides.

Tablets and Headphones: Load tablets with movies, games, and educational apps. Headphones are great for keeping the noise down and giving everyone some personal space.

Personal Experience: Bringing a tablet loaded with favorite movies and shows kept our kids entertained during a long flight. It made the journey much more pleasant for everyone.

Miscellaneous Items

A few additional items can make your trip more comfortable.

Reusable Water Bottles: Staying hydrated is important. We bring reusable water bottles that we can fill up throughout the day.

Daypack: A small daypack is perfect for carrying essentials like water bottles, snacks, a camera, and a jacket.

Snacks: Pack some favorite snacks for the trip. They're great for keeping everyone happy between meals and during outings.

Personal Story: On one trip, having a few granola bars and fruit snacks in my bag saved the day when the kids got hungry while we were out exploring.

Final Tips

Check the Weather: A week before your trip, start checking the weather forecast for London. This helps you pack appropriately for the conditions you'll face.

Leave Some Space: Try not to overpack. Leave a little space in your suitcase for any souvenirs or items you might buy during your trip.

Involve the Family: Get the whole family involved in packing. It teaches kids responsibility and ensures that everyone has what they need.

Packing for a family trip to London doesn't have to be stressful. With this essential packing list, you can feel confident that you have everything you need for a comfortable and enjoyable trip. Enjoy your time in this wonderful city!

Getting to London

Major Airports and How to Get to the City Train and Bus Options

When traveling to London, you'll likely arrive at one of the city's major airports. Knowing your options and how to navigate from the airport to the city center can make your arrival smooth and stress-free. Here's a detailed guide to help you get started.

London Heathrow Airport (LHR)

Heathrow is the largest and busiest airport in London, handling flights from all over the world. It's located about 15 miles west of central London.

Personal Experience: The first time we flew into Heathrow, I was amazed at how efficient the airport was despite its size. Everything from baggage claim to customs was well-organized.

Getting to the City

Heathrow Express: The fastest way to get to central London is the Heathrow Express train. It takes about 15 minutes to reach Paddington Station. The trains are comfortable, and there's plenty of space for luggage.

Underground (Tube): The Piccadilly Line offers a cheaper, though slower, option. It takes around 50 minutes to reach central London, but it's a direct route and convenient for those staying near Tube stations.

Taxi or Ride-Sharing: Taxis are available outside each terminal, and ride-sharing services like Uber operate from the airport. This option is more expensive but can be convenient, especially with lots of luggage or tired kids.

Bus and Coach: National Express coaches provide a budget-friendly option, connecting Heathrow to various parts of London and other cities. It's a slower option but useful for reaching specific destinations.

London Gatwick Airport (LGW)

Gatwick is the second-largest airport and is located about 30 miles south of central London. It's known for handling both international and budget airline flights.

Storytelling Moment: On our trip via Gatwick, we were pleasantly surprised by the airport's family-friendly facilities, including play areas and child-friendly restaurants.

Getting to the City

Gatwick Express: This non-stop train service to Victoria Station takes about 30 minutes. It's fast and efficient, especially for those staying in central London.

Trains: Regular trains also run to London Bridge and St Pancras International. They're slightly slower but offer more options depending on your destination.

Taxi or Ride-Sharing: Similar to Heathrow, taxis and ride-sharing services are readily available. We found it useful when traveling with kids and lots of luggage.

Bus and Coach: National Express and other coach services provide connections to various parts of London and beyond. It's a cost-effective option, though travel time can be longer.

London Stansted Airport (STN)

Stansted, located about 40 miles northeast of central London, is a hub for budget airlines like Ryanair and EasyJet.

Personal Touch: Arriving at Stansted, we appreciated the straightforward layout and efficient processing, which made getting out of the airport quick and easy.

Getting to the City

Stansted Express: This train service runs to Liverpool Street Station in about 45 minutes. It's the fastest way to reach central London and is very convenient.

Trains and Buses: Other train services and buses connect Stansted to various parts of London. Buses can be a good option if you're staying in specific neighborhoods.

Taxi or Ride-Sharing: Taxis and ride-sharing services are available but can be expensive given the distance to central London. We found this useful when we had an early morning flight and needed a reliable ride.

London Luton Airport (LTN)

Luton is another airport popular with budget airlines, situated about 35 miles north of central London.

Insider Tip: Luton can get busy, especially with budget travelers. Arriving early gives you enough time to navigate through the crowds and find your transport.

Getting to the City

Trains: Regular trains run to St Pancras International, taking around 25 minutes. A shuttle bus connects the airport to the Luton Airport Parkway station.

Buses: EasyBus and National Express offer direct bus services to various parts of London, which are budget-friendly though slower.

Taxi or Ride-Sharing: As with the other airports, taxis and ride-sharing options are available. They're convenient but can be costly.

London City Airport (LCY)

Located in East London, City Airport is the closest to central London and primarily serves business travelers and short-haul flights.

Personal Story: Flying into City Airport, we appreciated the quick and easy access to public transport, making it one of the most convenient airports for reaching the city center.

Getting to the City

DLR (Docklands Light Railway): The DLR connects the airport to the London Underground network. It's a quick and efficient way to reach central London.

Taxi or Ride-Sharing: Given the airport's proximity to the city, taxis and ride-sharing services are a convenient option and not as costly as from other airports.

Bus: Local buses also serve the airport, connecting to various parts of East London.

Final Tips for Getting to the City

Check Traffic: If you're taking a taxi or ride-sharing service, check traffic conditions as London traffic can be heavy, especially during peak hours.

Book in Advance: For trains and coaches, booking in advance can save you money and guarantee your seat, especially during busy travel periods.

Family-Friendly Services: Look out for family-friendly services like baby changing facilities, play areas, and priority boarding, which can make the airport experience smoother with kids.

Personal Story: On one trip, we pre-booked our train tickets from Gatwick, which not only saved us money but also ensured we had seats together as a family. It made the journey into the city much more comfortable.

By knowing your options and planning ahead, getting from London's major airports to the city center can be a smooth and hassle-free experience.

Navigating London with Kids

Exploring London with kids can be an exciting adventure, but it requires a bit of planning to ensure everyone has a great time. Here's a detailed guide on how to navigate the city with your little ones, packed with practical tips and personal experiences.

Using Public Transport

London's public transport system is extensive and family-friendly, making it easy to get around.

Personal Experience: On our first trip to London with the kids, we quickly realized how convenient the Tube is. The excitement on their faces as the train approached the platform was priceless.

The Underground (Tube)

Child-Friendly Routes: Most Tube stations are equipped with elevators and ramps, making it easier with strollers. Lines like the Jubilee and District are particularly accessible.

Oyster Cards: Get Oyster cards for everyone. Children under 11 travel free on the Tube, buses, and trams when accompanied by a paying adult. This made our travel budget-friendly and hassle-free.

Avoid Peak Hours: The Tube can get crowded during peak hours (7:30-9:30 AM and 5-7 PM). Traveling outside these times can make the journey more comfortable for kids.

Buses

Scenic Routes: London's iconic red buses offer a scenic way to see the city. The front seats on the upper deck provide a fantastic view, which our kids absolutely loved.

Accessibility: Buses are stroller-friendly, with designated spaces and ramps for easy boarding.

Personal Tip: We found that buses are great for shorter distances and offer a chance to rest while still seeing the city.

Walking Around

Walking is a great way to explore London's sights and sounds, especially with kids who need to burn off some energy.

Personal Story: One of our favorite memories is walking through Hyde Park. The kids enjoyed running around, and we had a lovely picnic by the Serpentine.

Walking Routes

Parks and Gardens: London's parks like Hyde Park, Regent's Park, and St. James's Park are perfect for leisurely walks and playtime.

City Walks: Walking between attractions can be enjoyable. For example, it's a pleasant walk from the Tower of London to the Tower Bridge and then along the South Bank.

Safety Tips

Hold Hands: Busy streets can be overwhelming. Holding hands and using strollers for younger children ensures they stay close.

Pedestrian Crossings: Use designated crossings and wait for the green man signal. Teaching kids about road safety is crucial.

Taxi and Ride-Sharing

Sometimes, especially after a long day, taking a taxi or ride-sharing service like Uber can be the most convenient option.

Insider Tip: Black cabs are spacious and can accommodate strollers and luggage easily. Plus, the drivers are knowledgeable and can provide tips on the best routes.

Ride-Sharing Services

Family-Friendly Options: Some ride-sharing services offer larger vehicles, perfect for families. We used these a few times when the kids were tired, and it was worth the extra cost for the convenience.

Personal Story: After a late-night show, we opted for a ride-share back to our hotel. The kids fell asleep in the car, making it a peaceful end to a busy day.

Attractions and Activities

Navigating to and within London's attractions can be made smoother with a bit of planning.

Museums and Galleries

Family-Friendly Museums: Places like the Natural History Museum and the Science Museum are designed with families in mind. They have interactive exhibits and plenty of rest areas.

Timed Entries: Booking timed entry tickets can reduce waiting times. We found this particularly useful at the popular attractions where lines can be long.

Outdoor Activities

Playgrounds: Many parks have excellent playgrounds. The Diana Memorial Playground in Kensington Gardens is a favorite, themed around Peter Pan with plenty of fun structures.

Boat Rides: Thames river cruises or pedalo boating in Hyde Park can be a fun break from walking.

Food and Rest Stops

Keeping kids fed and rested is key to a successful day out.

Eating Out

Family-Friendly Restaurants: London has a plethora of restaurants that cater to families. Chains like Pizza Express and Giraffe offer kids' menus and activity packs.

Picnics: On nice days, picnicking in a park can be a delightful and budget-friendly option. We loved our picnic at Greenwich Park, with stunning views over the city.

Rest Stops

Cafes and Libraries: Many cafes and libraries have cozy corners where you can rest. The Southbank Centre has a family-friendly area with comfortable seating.

Play Areas: Some larger stores and museums have play areas where kids can unwind. The LEGO Store in Leicester Square even has a play area that kept our kids entertained for a good hour.

Final Tips for Navigating with Kids

Plan Ahead: Before you head out, plan your route and check for any potential disruptions on public transport. Apps like Citymapper are incredibly useful for real-time updates.

Pack Smart: Carry a small backpack with essentials like snacks, water, wipes, and a change of clothes. A lightweight stroller can be a lifesaver for younger children.

Involve the Kids: Get the kids excited by involving them in the planning. Let them pick a couple of attractions they'd like to see each day. It keeps them engaged and looking forward to the adventure.

Personal Story: On our trip, letting the kids choose activities like visiting the London Zoo and taking a ride on the London Eye made them feel included and excited about each day's plans.

Accommodation

Family-Friendly Hotels

Finding the perfect place to stay is crucial for a successful family trip to London. The city offers a wide range of family-friendly hotels that cater to all needs and budgets. Here's a guide to help you choose the best accommodation for your family, based on my own experiences and research.

Central Locations

Staying in central London can be incredibly convenient for sightseeing and accessing public transport.

Personal Experience: On our first trip, we chose a hotel in Covent Garden. The central location made it easy to walk to major attractions like the British Museum and the West End theatres. The kids loved being so close to the action.

Recommended Hotels

The Strand Palace Hotel: Located in the heart of the West End, this hotel offers family rooms and special packages that include breakfast. It's just a short walk to Trafalgar Square and Covent Garden.

Premier Inn London County Hall: Adjacent to the London Eye and the South Bank, this hotel provides spacious family rooms and excellent service at a reasonable price.

Budget-Friendly Options

If you're traveling on a budget, there are plenty of affordable hotels that don't compromise on comfort.

Insider Tip: We found that booking well in advance can secure better rates, and many budget hotels offer deals for extended stays or family packages.

Recommended Hotels

Travelodge London Central: With multiple locations across the city, Travelodge offers clean, comfortable rooms at a great price. Their family rooms include extra beds and cribs on request.

Ibis London Blackfriars: This modern hotel offers competitive rates and is conveniently located near public transport. The family rooms are cozy, and the breakfast buffet is a hit with kids.

Luxury Stays

For those looking to splurge, London has several luxury hotels that cater exceptionally well to families.

Personal Story: We once treated ourselves to a stay at The Ritz for a special occasion. The staff went out of their way to make our kids feel welcome, providing them with activity packs and even organizing a treasure hunt in the hotel.

Recommended Hotels

The Ritz London: Known for its elegance and impeccable service, The Ritz offers family suites and a range of activities for children. Afternoon tea at The Ritz is a delightful experience for the whole family.

The Langham: Located near Regent's Park, The Langham offers luxurious family rooms and suites, along with a children's concierge service that arranges family-friendly activities and outings.

Unique and Quirky Stays

For a memorable experience, consider staying in one of London's unique accommodations.

Personal Touch: During one trip, we stayed on a houseboat on the Thames. It was an unforgettable experience that the kids still talk about.

Recommended Options

Houseboat Rentals: Websites like Airbnb offer houseboats that provide a unique way to experience London. These come equipped with all modern amenities and offer a cozy, adventurous stay.

ZSL London Zoo Lodges: For a truly unique experience, consider staying overnight at the zoo. The lodges are comfortable and provide exclusive after-hours access to the zoo, along with special tours.

Amenities to Look For

When choosing a family-friendly hotel, certain amenities can make your stay more comfortable and enjoyable.

Family Rooms and Suites: Look for hotels that offer spacious family rooms or suites with separate sleeping areas. This extra space is invaluable for families.

Kitchenette or Kitchen Access: Having the ability to prepare simple meals can save money and make meal times more convenient, especially with picky eaters.

Child-Friendly Facilities

Cribs and Extra Beds: Ensure the hotel can provide cribs or extra beds if needed.

High Chairs and Baby Monitors: These can be very helpful if you're traveling with infants or toddlers.

Play Areas and Pools: Hotels with play areas or swimming pools can keep kids entertained during downtime.

Personal Story: At one hotel, the kids were thrilled to find a playroom stocked with toys and games. It gave them a place to unwind and meet other children, which was a nice break from sightseeing.

Dining Options

Having good dining options either within the hotel or nearby can make mealtimes stress-free.

In-House Restaurants: Many family-friendly hotels offer in-house restaurants with kids' menus and flexible dining hours. This is convenient for breakfast before heading out for the day.

Nearby Eateries: Check if there are family-friendly restaurants or cafes within walking distance. This can be particularly useful if you return to the hotel late and need a quick meal.

Personal Touch: We loved staying at a hotel near Borough Market. Having access to fresh food and a variety of dining options was a treat, especially after a long day of exploring.

Final Tips for Choosing Family-Friendly Hotels

Book Early: Family rooms can fill up quickly, especially during peak travel seasons. Booking early ensures you get the best selection and rates.

Read Reviews: Websites like TripAdvisor and Booking.com offer detailed reviews from other families. These can provide insights into the hotel's amenities and service.

Ask for Recommendations: Don't hesitate to ask friends or family who have visited London for their recommendations. Personal experiences can often highlight the best places to stay.

Personal Story: A friend recommended a small boutique hotel that wasn't widely known but turned out to be perfect for our family. It had a warm, welcoming atmosphere and catered wonderfully to children.

Apartments and Vacation Rentals

When traveling to London with your family, choosing an apartment or vacation rental can offer more space, flexibility, and a homey feel compared to traditional hotels.

Benefits of Apartments and Vacation Rentals

Staying in an apartment or vacation rental comes with several advantages, especially for families.

Space and Privacy: Apartments typically offer more space than hotel rooms, giving everyone a bit more room to relax. Separate bedrooms and living areas provide much-needed privacy and comfort.

Personal Experience: During one of our trips, we stayed in a lovely two-bedroom apartment in South Kensington. Having separate bedrooms meant the kids could go to bed early, and we could enjoy some quiet time in the living room.

Kitchen Facilities: Having a kitchen allows you to prepare your own meals, which can be a big cost-saver and is particularly helpful for families with picky eaters or dietary restrictions.

Insider Tip: We loved shopping at local markets like Borough Market and cooking some of our meals at the apartment. It was a great way to experience local flavors and save money.

Laundry Facilities: Many vacation rentals come with washing machines and dryers, making it easier to pack light and keep everyone's clothes clean.

Personal Story: On a longer stay, having laundry facilities in our rental was a game-changer. It meant fewer clothes to pack and the convenience of fresh outfits without the cost of hotel laundry services.

Finding the Perfect Rental

Choosing the right apartment or vacation rental involves considering a few key factors.

Location: Look for rentals that are close to public transport, major attractions, and family-friendly amenities like parks and grocery stores.

Personal Touch: We once stayed in an apartment near Covent Garden. The central location made it easy to walk to the main sights, and having a playground nearby was perfect for the kids.

Reviews and Ratings: Read reviews from previous guests to get an idea of the rental's condition, the host's responsiveness, and the neighborhood's suitability for families.

Insider Tip: Websites like Airbnb, Vrbo, and Booking.com provide detailed reviews and ratings. Pay attention to comments about cleanliness, safety, and family-friendliness.

Amenities

Kitchen Essentials: Ensure the kitchen is well-equipped with basic cooking utensils, a stove, refrigerator, and microwave.

Child-Friendly Items: Check if the rental offers items like high chairs, cribs, and toys. Some hosts provide these upon request.

Wi-Fi and Entertainment: Reliable Wi-Fi is essential for planning your days and keeping everyone entertained. Look for rentals with TVs, books, or games.

Recommended Areas for Family Rentals

London has several neighborhoods that are particularly well-suited for families.

South Kensington

Benefits: Close to major museums like the Natural History Museum and the Science Museum, beautiful parks, and excellent transport links.

Personal Story: Staying in South Kensington, we enjoyed the quiet, residential feel while still being close to attractions. The kids loved the local playgrounds and the easy access to Hyde Park.

Greenwich

Benefits: A bit further from the hustle and bustle, Greenwich offers spacious rentals, beautiful parks, and the charming Greenwich Market.

Personal Experience: Our stay in Greenwich felt like a retreat. The slower pace and open spaces were perfect for our family, and the quick train ride into central London made sightseeing easy.

Notting Hill

Benefits: Known for its picturesque streets, family-friendly cafes, and the famous Portobello Road Market.

Insider Tip: We stayed in a charming Notting Hill apartment that had a cozy backyard. The kids enjoyed the outdoor space, and we loved the vibrant, eclectic neighborhood.

Booking Tips

When booking an apartment or vacation rental, a few strategies can ensure a smooth experience.

Book Early: Popular rentals can book up quickly, especially during peak travel seasons. Booking well in advance gives you more options and better rates.

Communicate with the Host: Reach out to the host with any questions before booking. This can include inquiries about check-in procedures, amenities, and local tips.

Personal Story: We once had a fantastic host who provided a detailed guidebook with local restaurant recommendations, public transport tips, and even a list of nearby playgrounds. It made our stay so much more enjoyable.

Check Policies: Understand the cancellation policy, house rules, and any additional fees (like cleaning fees or security deposits) before confirming your booking.

Making the Most of Your Stay

Once you've found the perfect rental, here are some tips to maximize your stay.

Settle In: Upon arrival, take some time to settle in and make the space feel like home. Unpack, stock the kitchen with groceries, and familiarize yourself with the appliances and amenities.

Explore the Neighborhood: Take a walk around your neighborhood to find nearby parks, cafes, and grocery stores. This helps you get a feel for the area and discover local gems.

Personal Touch: One of our favorite routines was grabbing breakfast pastries from a local bakery each morning. It became a special part of our trip that we all looked forward to.

Safety First: Ensure the rental is safe for kids by checking for potential hazards. Childproofing items like outlet covers and stair gates can be helpful if you're traveling with young children.

Local Experiences: Use the opportunity to live like a local. Visit neighborhood markets, attend community events, and interact with locals to enrich your travel experience.

Final Tip: Keep a list of emergency contacts, including the host's number, local hospitals, and emergency services. Having this information readily available provides peace of mind.

Unique Stays (Houseboats, Historic Homes)

For a truly memorable experience, consider staying in one of London's unique accommodations, such as houseboats or historic homes.

These options offer a distinct charm and an opportunity to see the city from a different perspective. Here's a detailed guide to help you choose the best unique stay for your family, filled with personal experiences and practical tips.

Houseboats on the Thames

Staying on a houseboat offers a unique way to experience London, combining the comforts of home with the novelty of being on the water.

Personal Experience: One of our most unforgettable stays was on a houseboat moored along the Thames. Waking up to the gentle rocking of the boat and the sight of swans gliding by was magical for the kids and relaxing for us.

Benefits of Houseboats

Scenic Views: Enjoy stunning views of the river and cityscape right from your deck. It's a peaceful retreat from the hustle and bustle of the city.

Cozy and Comfortable: Houseboats are often well-equipped with modern amenities, providing a cozy, home-like atmosphere. We had a fully equipped kitchen, a comfortable living area, and even a small deck for outdoor meals.

Unique Experience: The novelty of staying on a boat is exciting for kids and adults alike. It's an adventure they'll remember for years.

Recommended Houseboats

The Boathouse London: This luxurious floating home offers modern amenities, beautiful interiors, and stunning views. It's perfect for families looking for a unique yet comfortable stay.

The Harpy Houseboat: Moored at St. Katharine Docks, this historic barge offers a charming stay with easy access to the Tower of London and Tower Bridge.

Insider Tip: When booking a houseboat, check the location and accessibility. Some boats are moored in quieter areas, while others are closer to central attractions. Choose based on your family's preferences and itinerary.

Historic Homes

For a taste of history and elegance, consider staying in one of London's historic homes. These properties offer a unique blend of charm, character, and modern comforts.

Personal Story: We stayed in a beautifully restored Georgian townhouse in Bloomsbury. The history embedded in the walls and the period features, combined with modern amenities, made our stay both comfortable and fascinating.

Benefits of Historic Homes

Character and Charm: Historic homes are filled with unique architectural features, antique furnishings, and a sense of history that adds to the experience.

Spacious Living: These homes often offer more space than typical hotel rooms, with multiple bedrooms, living areas, and sometimes gardens.

Immersive Experience: Staying in a historic home provides a deeper connection to London's rich history and culture.

Recommended Historic Homes

Georgian Townhouses in Bloomsbury: Known for its literary history, Bloomsbury offers beautifully preserved Georgian townhouses that provide a charming and central base for exploring the city.

Victorian Homes in Kensington: These homes offer a glimpse into Victorian-era architecture and design. Staying here, we enjoyed the proximity to Kensington Gardens and the Natural History Museum.

Insider Tip: Look for historic homes that have been updated with modern conveniences like Wi-Fi, central heating, and fully equipped kitchens. This ensures a comfortable stay while still enjoying the historic ambiance.

Choosing the Right Unique Stay

When deciding between a houseboat and a historic home, consider the following factors.

Location: Houseboats are often located along the Thames or in quieter docks, providing a serene environment. Historic homes can be found in various neighborhoods, each offering different attractions and amenities.

Personal Experience: We loved the peacefulness of staying on the river, but also enjoyed the convenience of being in a central neighborhood when we stayed in a historic home.

Space and Amenities: Houseboats can be cozy but may have limited space compared to historic homes. Consider the size of your family and your need for space when choosing.

Unique Features: Houseboats offer the novelty of being on the water, which can be particularly exciting for kids. Historic homes provide a sense of stepping back in time, which can be educational and inspiring.

Insider Tip: For a truly memorable stay, consider splitting your time between a houseboat and a historic home. This allows you to experience the best of both worlds and adds variety to your trip.

Making the Most of Your Stay

To ensure a fantastic experience in your unique accommodation, here are some tips.

Prepare for the Environment: If staying on a houseboat, be mindful of the movement of the boat and the surrounding water. If your family includes members who are prone to motion sickness, pack remedies just in case.

Explore the Local Area: Both houseboats and historic homes are often located in picturesque or historically significant areas. Take the time to explore the local surroundings. For example, stroll along the Thames Path or visit nearby historical sites.

Personal Story: While staying in a houseboat, we enjoyed evening walks along the river and discovered charming riverside pubs and cafes. During our stay in a historic home, we visited the nearby British Museum and enjoyed the lush squares of Bloomsbury.

Respect the Property: These unique accommodations often come with specific rules to maintain their condition and historical integrity. Follow the guidelines provided by the host to ensure a respectful and enjoyable stay.

Final Tip: Keep a journal or take plenty of photos to capture the unique aspects of your stay. These memories will be cherished long after your trip is over.

Tips for Finding the Best Deals

Traveling to London with your family can be an incredible experience, and finding the best deals on accommodations, transportation, and attractions can make it even more enjoyable. Here are some practical tips and personal insights to help you save money while ensuring a fantastic trip.

Booking Accommodations

Finding affordable and comfortable accommodations is crucial for a successful family trip.

Personal Experience: On our last trip to London, we managed to find a great deal on a family-friendly hotel by booking well in advance. This allowed us to stay within our budget while enjoying a central location.

Early Booking

Plan Ahead: Booking your hotel or vacation rental several months in advance can often secure lower rates. Many properties offer early-bird discounts.

Flexibility with Dates: If your travel dates are flexible, you can often find better deals. Mid-week stays are typically cheaper than weekends.

Insider Tip: Use price comparison websites like Booking.com, Expedia, and Trivago to compare rates across different platforms. Sometimes, booking directly through the hotel's website can also yield special discounts or perks.

Last-Minute Deals

Mobile Apps: Apps like HotelTonight offer last-minute deals on hotel rooms. While it can be a bit of a gamble, the savings can be substantial.

Special Offers: Check for special promotions or package deals that include breakfast, parking, or tickets to local attractions. These can add significant value to your stay.

Personal Story: During one trip, we found a last-minute deal on a beautiful apartment in Notting Hill through Airbnb. It turned out to be one of the highlights of our trip, providing a cozy home base in a charming neighborhood.

Saving on Transportation

Navigating London can be costly, but there are ways to save on transportation.

Public Transport Passes

Oyster Card: Purchase an Oyster card for discounted fares on the Tube, buses, and other public transport. Kids under 11 travel free on the Tube and buses when accompanied by a paying adult.

Travelcards: If you plan to use public transport frequently, consider buying a Travelcard. It offers unlimited travel within specific zones and can be more economical than single fares.

Insider Tip: We always get Oyster cards for the family. They're convenient, and the fare capping system ensures we never overspend on daily travel.

Walking and Biking

Walk When Possible: London is a walkable city, and many attractions are within walking distance of each other. Walking not only saves money but also allows you to discover hidden gems along the way.

Bike Rentals: Santander Cycles (Boris Bikes) offer a fun and affordable way to get around. Kids will love the adventure, and it's a great way to see the city.

Personal Story: One of our favorite days was spent biking through Hyde Park and along the Thames. It was an inexpensive way to explore and provided plenty of opportunities for spontaneous picnics and playtime.

Dining on a Budget

Eating out in London can be expensive, but there are plenty of ways to enjoy delicious meals without breaking the bank.

Market Meals

Local Markets: Visit markets like Borough Market, Camden Market, and Portobello Road Market for affordable and diverse food options. These markets offer everything from street food to fresh produce.

Personal Experience: We often grab lunch at Borough Market. The kids love trying different foods, and we appreciate the variety and reasonable prices.

Restaurant Deals

Early Bird Specials: Many restaurants offer discounts for early diners. Look for early bird menus or pre-theatre specials.

Voucher Sites: Websites like Groupon and VoucherCodes offer discounts and deals for various restaurants. Check these sites before heading out to eat.

Self-Catering

Grocery Stores: If you're staying in an apartment or vacation rental, take advantage of having a kitchen by shopping at local grocery stores like Tesco, Sainsbury's, or Waitrose. Preparing some meals at home can significantly cut down on dining expenses.

Personal Story: During one trip, we stayed in an apartment and enjoyed cooking breakfast each morning. It was a fun family activity, and starting the day with a hearty, homemade meal saved us money.

Affordable Attractions

London has a wealth of free or low-cost attractions that are perfect for families.

Free Museums and Galleries

Museums: Many of London's top museums, including the British Museum, the Natural History Museum, and the Science Museum, offer free entry. These are fantastic places for kids to learn and explore without spending a penny.

Galleries: Art galleries like the National Gallery and Tate Modern are also free to enter and provide enriching experiences for the whole family.

Parks and Outdoor Spaces

Royal Parks: London's parks, such as Hyde Park, Regent's Park, and Kensington Gardens, offer beautiful green spaces for picnics, play, and relaxation.

Personal Touch: Our kids loved the Diana Memorial Playground in Kensington Gardens. It's free to enter and has fantastic play structures inspired by Peter Pan.

Discount Passes

London Pass: Consider purchasing the London Pass, which provides entry to multiple attractions at a discounted rate. It can be a cost-effective way to see the city's top sights.

2-for-1 Offers: If you're traveling by train, check out Days Out Guide, which offers 2-for-1 entry to many attractions when you show your train ticket.

Personal Story: We used the London Pass on one trip and found it saved us a lot on entry fees, plus it made planning our days much easier. We didn't have to worry about buying separate tickets for each attraction.

Final Tips for Finding Deals

Flexibility: Be flexible with your plans. Sometimes shifting your itinerary by a day or two can open up new deals and discounts.

Local Knowledge: Ask locals for recommendations. Sometimes the best deals aren't advertised online but are known by those who live in the area.

Personal Touch: On our first visit, a local café owner recommended a nearby restaurant that had a fantastic kids' menu and great prices. It ended up being one of our favorite dining experiences.

Stay Informed: Sign up for newsletters from travel deal websites and follow social media accounts that focus on London travel tips. They often share exclusive deals and last-minute offers.

Personal Story: I subscribed to a few travel deal newsletters, and through one, I discovered a flash sale on a family-friendly hotel. The savings allowed us to extend our trip by a day, giving us more time to explore the city.

Getting Around London
Public Transport

Navigating London's extensive public transport system can be a breeze with a little preparation. Here's a detailed guide to help you and your family make the most of London's public transport, filled with practical tips and personal experiences.

The Underground (Tube)

The London Underground, or the Tube, is the quickest way to get around the city. With 11 lines covering the entire metropolitan area, it's an efficient mode of transport for families.

Personal Experience: On our first day in London, we took the Tube from Heathrow to our hotel in central London. The kids were excited to ride the trains, and we found it to be a fast and convenient way to travel.

Tips for Using the Tube

Oyster Cards: Purchase an Oyster card for each adult. Kids under 11 travel free on the Tube, buses, and trams when accompanied by a paying adult. The cards offer the best fares and can be used on multiple types of public transport.

Contactless Payment: If you don't have an Oyster card, contactless payment cards and devices are also accepted. They offer the same discounted fares.

Plan Your Route: Use apps like Citymapper or the TfL (Transport for London) website to plan your route and check for any service updates or disruptions.

Insider Tip: Travel during off-peak hours (outside 7:30-9:30 AM and 5-7 PM) to avoid the crowds and ensure a more comfortable journey.

Buses

London's iconic red buses are a great way to see the city and travel shorter distances.

Personal Story: One of our favorite memories was riding the top deck of a double-decker bus through central London. The kids loved the view, and it gave us a different perspective of the city.

Tips for Using Buses

Routes and Stops: Bus routes cover areas that the Tube doesn't, making them useful for reaching more specific destinations. Bus stops are marked with red signs and route numbers.

Oyster and Contactless: The same Oyster card or contactless payment method used on the Tube works for buses. Remember to tap in when boarding.

Bus Maps: Pick up a bus map or use online resources to familiarize yourself with the routes and stops near your accommodation and attractions.

Insider Tip: Sit on the upper deck at the front for the best views, especially on routes that pass major landmarks like the 9, 11, and 15.

Docklands Light Railway (DLR)

The DLR is an automated light metro system serving the Docklands area and East London. It's particularly useful for reaching attractions like the O2 Arena and Greenwich.

Personal Experience: We used the DLR to visit the Cutty Sark and Greenwich Observatory. The kids were fascinated by the driverless trains, and it was an easy and scenic journey.

Tips for Using the DLR

Oyster and Contactless: The DLR accepts Oyster cards and contactless payments. Travel zones and fare structures are the same as the Tube.

Seating: Sit at the front for a "driver's-eye view," which can be especially exciting for children.

Overground and National Rail

The London Overground and various National Rail services connect the outer boroughs and suburbs to central London.

Insider Tip: We took the Overground to visit friends in North London. It was less crowded than the Tube and offered a smooth ride through some picturesque neighborhoods.

Tips for Using Overground and Rail

Oyster and Contactless: These services also accept Oyster cards and contactless payments, making it easy to switch between different transport modes.

Planning Routes: Use National Rail Enquiries or TfL for schedules and route planning. Overground maps are available at stations and online.

Trams

Trams serve South London, primarily around Croydon and Wimbledon. While less extensive than other modes, they're efficient for local travel in those areas.

Tips for Using Trams

Oyster and Contactless: Trams accept the same payment methods, and children under 11 travel free.

Routes: Check tram maps and schedules if your itinerary includes South London attractions.

River Services

River buses and cruises along the Thames offer a unique way to see the city and avoid road traffic.

Personal Story: We took a Thames Clipper from the London Eye to Greenwich. It was a relaxing journey with stunning views of the city's landmarks from the water.

Tips for Using River Services

Tickets: Oyster cards are accepted on Thames Clippers, but not on tourist cruises. Check the specific operator's requirements.

Routes and Timetables: River services run on set schedules and routes, so plan ahead to fit them into your itinerary.

Practical Tips for Families

Plan Ahead: Use travel apps and maps to plan your routes and check for any service changes or delays. Knowing your stops and connections in advance makes the journey smoother.

Pack Essentials: Bring water, snacks, and entertainment for the kids, especially for longer journeys. A small backpack with these essentials can make a big difference.

Accessibility: Most stations have step-free access and facilities for strollers and wheelchairs. Check the TfL website for detailed accessibility information for each station.

Safety First: Hold hands and keep an eye on your belongings, especially in busy stations and on crowded trains. Teach kids to stay close and recognize landmarks or signs near your accommodation.

Personal Story: On our first trip, we made a game of spotting the different Tube line colors on maps. It kept the kids engaged and helped them learn about navigating the city.

Using London's public transport can be an efficient and enjoyable way to explore the city with your family. With a bit of preparation and these practical tips, you'll be able to travel like a local and make the most of your time in this vibrant city.

Walking and Biking

Exploring London on foot or by bike is a fantastic way to soak in the city's sights, sounds, and atmosphere. It allows for spontaneous discoveries and offers a more intimate experience of the city's vibrant neighborhoods and iconic landmarks.

Walking in London

Walking is one of the best ways to explore London's diverse neighborhoods and famous landmarks. It's free, healthy, and gives you the flexibility to stop and enjoy sights at your own pace.

Personal Experience: Our family loves walking through London's various districts. One of our favorite walks was from Trafalgar Square to Buckingham Palace, passing through St. James's Park. The kids enjoyed feeding the ducks, and we all appreciated the fresh air and beautiful scenery.

Tips for Walking in London

Plan Your Routes: Use maps and travel apps to plan your walking routes. Some of our favorite walking routes include the South Bank from the London Eye to Tower Bridge, and the route through Covent Garden to the British Museum.

Comfortable Footwear: Wear comfortable shoes suitable for long walks. We learned the hard way that fashionable shoes are not always practical for a day of sightseeing!

Layered Clothing: London weather can be unpredictable, so dress in layers and bring a waterproof jacket. An umbrella is also handy to have.

Stay Hydrated and Fed: Carry water bottles and snacks, especially if you're out with kids. We always pack some granola bars and fruit to keep the kids energized.

Safety: Hold hands with younger children, especially when crossing busy streets. Use pedestrian crossings and follow traffic signals.

Engaging Routes

The South Bank Walk: Start at the London Eye and walk along the Thames, passing landmarks like the Tate Modern, Shakespeare's Globe, and Tower Bridge. There are plenty of cafes and attractions along the way to keep everyone entertained.

Regent's Park to Camden Market: Begin at Regent's Park, enjoy the open spaces and playgrounds, then head to Camden Market for a lively mix of food stalls, shops, and street performers.

Hyde Park and Kensington Gardens: These adjacent parks offer beautiful walking paths, playgrounds, and landmarks like the Serpentine Lake and Kensington Palace. The Diana Memorial Playground is a hit with kids.

Personal Story: One afternoon, we took a leisurely walk from the Tower of London to the Tower Bridge and then strolled along the South Bank. The kids loved watching the street performers, and we enjoyed a relaxing coffee break with views of the river.

Biking in London

Biking is a fun and efficient way to explore London, providing a different perspective of the city and access to areas not easily reached by car or public transport.

Personal Experience: Renting bikes and cycling through Hyde Park was one of our family's highlights. The wide paths and beautiful scenery made it a perfect family activity, and the kids enjoyed the freedom of riding their bikes in such a large, open space.

Tips for Biking in London

Bike Rentals: Use Santander Cycles (also known as Boris Bikes) for convenient bike rentals. These bikes are available at docking stations throughout the city and can be rented for short periods. Alternatively, some companies offer rentals for a day or longer.

Safety Gear: Always wear helmets and ensure bikes are fitted with lights, especially if you're cycling in the evening. We brought our own helmets, but rentals usually provide them as well.

Bike Lanes and Routes: Stick to designated bike lanes and routes. London has an expanding network of cycle superhighways and quietways that are safer and more pleasant for cyclists.

Respect Traffic Rules: Follow all traffic signals and signs. Teach kids the basics of road safety and ensure they are comfortable riding in an urban environment.

Family-Friendly Cycling Routes

Hyde Park and Kensington Gardens: These parks offer flat, wide paths that are ideal for cycling. The Serpentine Road in Hyde Park is particularly scenic.

Regent's Canal: Cycle along the canal from Little Venice to Camden Market. The route is mostly flat and passes through picturesque areas with plenty of stops for refreshments.

Richmond Park: This large park in southwest London is perfect for a day out on bikes. The park has cycling paths and is home to herds of deer, making it a unique and memorable experience.

Personal Story: We spent a day cycling in Richmond Park, where the kids were thrilled to see deer up close. We packed a picnic and enjoyed a leisurely lunch in the park, which was a wonderful way to spend time together as a family.

Combining Walking and Biking

Combining walking and biking can maximize your exploration and keep things interesting for the kids.

Mixed Itineraries

Walk and Bike: Walk to a destination and then rent bikes to explore further. For instance, walk through Covent Garden, then rent bikes to cycle along the Thames.

Park Exploration: Spend the morning walking through a park, then rent bikes to cover more ground in the afternoon.

Final Tips

Plan Breaks: Schedule regular breaks for snacks, rest, and play. Parks and cafes make excellent stopovers.

Interactive Maps: Use interactive maps and apps to find the best walking and biking routes. These tools can also help locate nearby attractions and rest spots.

Engage the Kids: Involve the kids in planning the route and choosing destinations. It keeps them engaged and excited about the day's activities.

Personal Story: One of our best days involved a morning walk through the streets of Soho, followed by a bike ride through Regent's Park. We finished the day with a boat ride on the Serpentine Lake, making it a perfect blend of activities.

Family-Friendly Transportation Options

Traveling around London with children can be a breeze if you choose the right transportation options. From iconic double-decker buses to child-friendly taxis, London offers a variety of family-friendly ways to get around.

The Underground (Tube)

The London Underground, or the Tube, is one of the fastest ways to travel across the city, and it's generally quite family-friendly.

Personal Experience: On our first visit, we relied heavily on the Tube. The kids found it exciting to travel underground and spot the different line colors on the maps.

Tips for Using the Tube with Kids

Oyster Cards: Get an Oyster card for each adult. Children under 11 travel free on the Tube when accompanied by a paying adult. This makes the Tube a cost-effective option for families.

Accessibility: Many stations have lifts and escalators, making it easier to navigate with strollers. However, some older stations may not be fully accessible, so check ahead if you need step-free access.

Avoid Peak Times: Travel outside of peak hours (7:30-9:30 AM and 5-7 PM) to avoid crowded trains and platforms.

Insider Tip: Plan your route in advance using the TfL website or apps like Citymapper to ensure you take the most convenient and accessible path.

Buses

London's iconic red double-decker buses are not only a practical way to get around but also a fun experience for kids.

Personal Story: We took a double-decker bus to explore central London. Sitting on the top deck gave us a fantastic view of the city, and the kids loved spotting landmarks from above.

Tips for Using Buses with Kids

Routes and Stops: Buses cover routes that the Tube doesn't, making them useful for reaching specific destinations. Bus stops are clearly marked, and routes are easy to follow.

Oyster and Contactless: Use your Oyster card or contactless payment method for bus fares. Children under 11 travel free on buses.

Stroller-Friendly: Buses have designated spaces for strollers and wheelchairs. You can board with your stroller without having to fold it, which is convenient for parents.

Insider Tip: The front seats on the top deck offer the best views and are a hit with kids. Popular routes like the 9, 11, and 15 pass by many major landmarks.

Taxis and Ride-Sharing

Sometimes, taking a taxi or using a ride-sharing service is the most convenient option, especially when traveling with young children or lots of luggage.

Personal Experience: After a long day of sightseeing, we opted for an Uber back to our hotel. It was a relief to have a door-to-door service, and the kids could rest during the ride.

Tips for Using Taxis and Ride-Sharing with Kids

Black Cabs: London's black cabs are spacious and can accommodate strollers and luggage. They're also equipped with ramps for wheelchair access.

Ride-Sharing Apps: Services like Uber offer family-friendly options, including larger vehicles for groups. You can request a car with a child seat if needed.

Safety: Always ensure that children are seated safely with appropriate child seats. Some taxis and ride-sharing services provide these upon request.

Insider Tip: Use apps to book your ride in advance, especially during busy times. This ensures you have a vehicle ready when you need it.

River Services

Traveling by boat along the Thames can be both a practical and scenic way to get around, offering a unique perspective of the city.

Personal Story: We took a Thames Clipper from the London Eye to Greenwich. It was a relaxing journey with stunning views of the city's landmarks, and the kids were thrilled to be on a boat.

Tips for Using River Services with Kids

Oyster and Contactless: Thames Clippers accept Oyster cards and contactless payments, making it easy to hop on and off.

Family Tickets: Look for family ticket options that offer discounted rates. Some services provide free travel for young children.

Comfort and Amenities: River buses are comfortable and often have indoor seating, restrooms, and snack bars.

Insider Tip: Choose a route that passes by major landmarks like Tower Bridge, the Tower of London, and the Houses of Parliament for an unforgettable sightseeing experience.

Cycling

Biking is a fun and active way to explore London, especially in its many parks and dedicated cycling routes.

Personal Experience: We rented bikes and cycled through Hyde Park. The kids loved the freedom of biking in such a large, open space, and it was a great way to see the park's attractions.

Tips for Biking with Kids

Bike Rentals: Use Santander Cycles for convenient bike rentals. There are docking stations throughout the city, and the bikes are easy to use.

Safety Gear: Always wear helmets and ensure bikes are equipped with lights. Rentals usually include these, but it's good to check.

Child Seats: If you're biking with younger children, look for bikes with child seats or trailers.

Insider Tip: Stick to parks and designated cycling paths to avoid busy streets. Hyde Park, Regent's Park, and Richmond Park offer beautiful and safe biking routes.

Trams and DLR

Trams and the Docklands Light Railway (DLR) are less commonly used but are excellent options for certain areas.

Tips for Using Trams and DLR with Kids

Oyster and Contactless: These services accept Oyster cards and contactless payments. Children under 11 travel free.

Driverless Trains: The DLR is particularly fun for kids because they can sit at the front and pretend to drive the train.

Insider Tip: Use the DLR to reach attractions like the Cutty Sark, the National Maritime Museum, and the O2 Arena. It's a smooth and scenic ride through the Docklands area.

Practical Tips for Family-Friendly Transport

Plan Ahead: Use apps like Citymapper or the TfL website to plan your routes and check for any service updates or delays.

Pack Essentials: Bring a small backpack with water, snacks, and entertainment for the kids, especially for longer journeys.

Stay Safe: Hold hands with younger children, especially in crowded areas and while crossing streets. Teach older kids to recognize landmarks or signs near your accommodation.

Personal Story: On one trip, we made a game of spotting the different Tube line colors on maps, which kept the kids engaged and helped them learn about navigating the city.

Top Attractions for Families

Historical Sites Tower of London, Buckingham Palace

London is rich with historical sites that offer fascinating glimpses into the past. Two of the most iconic landmarks are the Tower of London and Buckingham Palace. Here's a detailed guide to visiting these incredible sites with your family, ensuring a memorable and educational experience.

Tower of London

The Tower of London is a historic fortress located on the north bank of the River Thames. It has served as a royal palace, prison, treasury, and even a zoo. Visiting the Tower is like stepping back in time, and there's plenty to see and do for families.

Personal Experience: Our visit to the Tower of London was a highlight of our trip. The kids were captivated by the stories of kings and queens, and the sight of the Crown Jewels left us all in awe.

Highlights of the Tower of London

The Crown Jewels: One of the main attractions, the Crown Jewels are a dazzling display of royal regalia, including crowns, scepters, and orbs. The kids were amazed by the sparkling jewels and the history behind them.

The White Tower: The central keep of the Tower, built by William the Conqueror, houses an impressive collection of arms and armor. We enjoyed exploring the exhibits and learning about medieval warfare.

Yeoman Warder Tours: Also known as Beefeaters, the Yeoman Warders provide guided tours filled with entertaining and informative stories about the Tower's history. Our guide's humorous anecdotes kept the kids engaged and entertained.

Ravens: According to legend, if the ravens ever leave the Tower, the kingdom will fall. Seeing these majestic birds up close was a treat for the kids, who loved hearing the myths surrounding them.

Practical Tips

Book Tickets in Advance: To avoid long lines, purchase your tickets online ahead of time. This also gives you access to special offers and family tickets.

Arrive Early: The Tower opens at 9:00 AM. Arriving early helps you beat the crowds and have a more relaxed experience.

Explore the Grounds: There's plenty to see outside the main buildings, including the medieval palace, the battlements, and the Tower Green where famous executions took place.

Personal Story: One of our favorite moments was walking along the ancient walls and imagining life in medieval times. The kids were particularly fascinated by the stories of the princes in the Tower.

Buckingham Palace

Buckingham Palace is the official residence of the British monarch. It's not only a symbol of the British monarchy but also a working royal palace. Visiting Buckingham Palace offers a glimpse into the life of the royal family and the grandeur of British royalty.

Personal Experience: Watching the Changing of the Guard at Buckingham Palace was a thrilling experience for our family. The pageantry and precision of the ceremony were truly impressive.

Highlights of Buckingham Palace

Changing of the Guard: This iconic ceremony takes place daily during the summer and every other day in the winter. It's a must-see event, featuring soldiers in traditional red tunics and bearskin hats. Arrive early to get a good viewing spot.

State Rooms: During the summer months, the State Rooms of Buckingham Palace are open to the public. These lavishly decorated rooms are used for official ceremonies and entertaining guests. We marveled at the opulence and the priceless artworks on display.

The Royal Mews: This working stables complex houses the royal collection of historic coaches and carriages, including the magnificent Gold State Coach. The kids were fascinated by the grandeur and history of the royal vehicles.

The Queen's Gallery: This art gallery features changing exhibitions from the Royal Collection. It's a great way to see world-class art and artifacts in a regal setting.

Practical Tips

Check the Schedule: The Changing of the Guard schedule can vary, so check the official website before planning your visit. The ceremony usually starts at 11:00 AM.

Book State Rooms Tickets in Advance: If you're visiting during the summer, book your tickets for the State Rooms early. Guided tours are available and provide a richer understanding of the palace's history and function.

Plan for Security Checks: Allow extra time for security checks, especially if you're visiting the State Rooms or attending the Changing of the Guard.

Personal Story: During our visit, we took a stroll through St. James's Park, located just opposite the palace. The kids loved the playground and watching the pelicans, while we enjoyed the beautiful gardens and the view of the palace.

Combining Your Visit

Both the Tower of London and Buckingham Palace offer rich historical experiences that can be enjoyed in a single day or over separate days, depending on your schedule.

Sample Itinerary

Morning: Start your day at the Tower of London. Arrive early to explore the Crown Jewels and take a Yeoman Warder tour. Enjoy a walk along the battlements and see the ravens.

Lunch: Have lunch at one of the cafes near the Tower or bring a picnic to enjoy by the river.

Afternoon: Head to Buckingham Palace for the Changing of the Guard. If visiting during the summer, tour the State Rooms and the Royal Mews. Finish with a relaxing walk through St. James's Park.

Personal Touch: We found that breaking up our visit with a leisurely lunch and some downtime in the park made the day more enjoyable for everyone, especially the kids.

Final Tips for Visiting Historical Sites

Engage the Kids: Use storytelling and fun facts to make history come alive for the kids. Many attractions offer family-friendly tours and activity packs that can help engage younger visitors.

Comfortable Footwear: Both the Tower of London and Buckingham Palace involve a lot of walking. Wear comfortable shoes to keep everyone happy and energetic.

Stay Hydrated and Snack Smart: Carry water bottles and snacks to keep the kids hydrated and satisfied throughout the day.

Photography: Bring a camera or smartphone to capture the memories. Both sites offer plenty of photo opportunities, from the grandeur of Buckingham Palace to the historic ambiance of the Tower of London.

Museums: Natural History Museum, Science Museum

London is home to some of the world's most famous museums, perfect for family visits. The Natural History Museum and the Science Museum, located in South Kensington, offer engaging and educational experiences for all ages. Here's a detailed guide to making the most of your visit to these incredible institutions.

Natural History Museum

The Natural History Museum is a treasure trove of natural wonders, featuring everything from dinosaur skeletons to precious gems. It's an ideal destination for curious minds and budding scientists.

Personal Experience**: Our visit to the Natural History Museum was one of the highlights of our trip. The kids were fascinated by the life-sized dinosaur skeletons and interactive exhibits.

Highlights of the Natural History Museum

Dinosaurs: The Dinosaur Gallery is a must-see. It features a towering T-Rex and a range of other dinosaur skeletons and fossils. The animatronic T-Rex was a particular favorite with our kids.

Hintze Hall: The grand entrance hall houses a stunning blue whale skeleton suspended from the ceiling. It's an awe-inspiring sight and a great spot for photos.

Earth Hall: Explore the wonders of our planet, including the Earthquake Simulator, where you can experience what it feels like to be in an earthquake. The kids loved the immersive experience.

Creepy Crawlies: This section features live insects and arachnids, as well as detailed displays about their habitats and behaviors. It's both educational and thrilling.

Practical Tips

Free Entry: Admission to the Natural History Museum is free, though donations are appreciated. Special exhibitions may require a ticket.

Arrive Early: To avoid the crowds, especially during weekends and school holidays, try to arrive early when the museum opens at 10:00 AM.

Interactive Guides: Pick up a map and family activity trails at the information desk. These guides are designed to make the visit more engaging for children.

Personal Story: One of the most memorable parts of our visit was the interactive butterfly exhibit, where the kids could get up close to live butterflies in a tropical environment. It was both fun and educational.

Science Museum

The Science Museum, located just next to the Natural History Museum, is packed with interactive exhibits and hands-on activities that bring science and technology to life.

Personal Experience: Our day at the Science Museum was filled with excitement and discovery. The kids were thrilled by the interactive exhibits and the IMAX theatre experience.

Highlights of the Science Museum

Wonderlab: This interactive gallery is designed to spark curiosity in children. With over 50 exhibits, live science shows, and demonstrations, it's a place where learning is fun and hands-on.

Exploring Space: This gallery showcases the history of space exploration, including real spacecraft and space suits. The kids were particularly fascinated by the Apollo 10 Command Module.

The Garden: Designed for younger children (ages 3-6), this interactive play area encourages exploration through water play, construction, and sensory activities. It's a great spot for little ones to learn through play.

Flight Gallery: This gallery features historic aircraft and aviation artifacts. The life-size planes suspended from the ceiling are impressive, and the interactive flight simulators are a hit with older kids.

Practical Tips

Free Entry: Admission to the Science Museum is free, though some special exhibitions and activities, like the Wonderlab, may require a ticket.

Pre-Book Activities: For popular attractions like the Wonderlab and the IMAX theater, it's a good idea to book tickets in advance to secure your spot and avoid long lines.

Plan Your Visit: The museum is large, so plan your visit around the exhibits that most interest your family. Use the museum's map to navigate and prioritize your must-see sections.

Personal Story: Our kids loved the IMAX theater, where we watched a documentary about space. The massive screen and immersive experience made them feel like they were traveling through the cosmos.

Combining Your Visit

The Natural History Museum and the Science Museum are conveniently located next to each other, making it easy to visit both in one day or over two days.

Sample Itinerary

Morning: Start your day at the Natural History Museum. Explore the Dinosaur Gallery and Hintze Hall. Take a break in the museum's cafe or bring snacks for a quick energy boost.

Lunch: Enjoy lunch at one of the nearby cafes or have a picnic in the beautiful Kensington Gardens, just a short walk away.

Afternoon: Head to the Science Museum. Begin with the Wonderlab and then explore the other galleries based on your family's interests. End the day with a show at the IMAX theater.

Personal Touch: We found that splitting our visit into two days allowed us to fully enjoy each museum without feeling rushed. It also gave the kids time to rest and absorb what they had learned.

Final Tips for Visiting Museums

Engage the Kids: Use interactive exhibits and hands-on activities to keep the kids engaged. Many museums offer special programs and workshops designed for children.

Comfortable Footwear: Both museums involve a lot of walking, so wear comfortable shoes to keep everyone happy and energetic.

Stay Hydrated and Snack Smart: Carry water bottles and snacks to keep the kids hydrated and satisfied throughout the day. Both museums have cafes, but having your own snacks can be convenient.

Photography: Bring a camera or smartphone to capture the memories. Both museums offer plenty of photo opportunities, from the grand architecture to the fascinating exhibits.

Visiting the Natural History Museum and the Science Museum provides a fun and educational experience for the whole family.

Parks and Outdoor Spaces: Hyde Park, Regent's Park, Kew Gardens

London's parks and outdoor spaces offer a breath of fresh air and a break from the bustling city streets. They provide a perfect setting for family activities, picnics, and leisurely strolls.

Hyde Park

Hyde Park is one of the largest and most famous parks in London, offering a wide range of activities and attractions for families.

Personal Experience: Hyde Park became our go-to spot for family picnics and leisurely walks. The kids loved feeding the ducks at the Serpentine Lake, and we enjoyed the peaceful green spaces.

Highlights of Hyde Park

The Serpentine: This large lake is perfect for boating and feeding the ducks. You can rent pedal boats and rowboats, which is a fun activity for families. There's also a swimming area for those warm summer days.

Diana Memorial Playground: Inspired by Peter Pan, this playground features a pirate ship, teepees, and various play structures. It's a fantastic spot for kids to burn off energy and use their imagination.

Speakers' Corner: Located at the northeast corner of the park, this historic spot is known for its open-air debates and public speaking. It's a unique cultural experience, though more interesting for older children and adults.

The Rose Garden: This beautifully landscaped garden is a peaceful place to stroll and enjoy the vibrant flowers. It's a great spot for some quiet time or a family photo.

Practical Tips

Bike Rentals: Hyde Park has dedicated cycling paths and offers bike rentals, including options for children. It's a fun way to explore the park and get some exercise.

Picnic Spots: Bring a picnic blanket and enjoy lunch on the grassy areas. The park has several cafes and kiosks, but packing your own snacks gives you more flexibility.

Seasonal Events: Check the park's schedule for seasonal events like concerts, festivals, and outdoor movies. These events can add an extra layer of excitement to your visit.

Personal Story: One sunny afternoon, we rented pedal boats on the Serpentine. The kids had a blast steering the boat, and we enjoyed the serene views of the park from the water.

Regent's Park

Regent's Park is another large park with beautifully manicured gardens, playgrounds, and even a zoo. It's a fantastic destination for families looking for a mix of relaxation and adventure.

Highlights of Regent's Park

Queen Mary's Gardens: Home to over 12,000 roses, this garden is a stunning display of color and fragrance. It's a perfect spot for a relaxing stroll or a family photo.

Regent's Park Boating Lake: Rent a paddle boat or a rowboat and enjoy a leisurely time on the water. It's a peaceful activity that's fun for all ages.

London Zoo: Located within the park, the London Zoo is home to a wide variety of animals and offers interactive exhibits and feeding sessions. It's a must-visit for families with kids.

Playgrounds: The park has several well-maintained playgrounds where kids can climb, swing, and play to their hearts' content.

Practical Tips

Zoo Tickets: Purchase tickets to the London Zoo in advance to avoid long lines and secure your preferred time slot.

Cafes and Picnics: There are several cafes in the park, but packing a picnic allows for a flexible and relaxed meal. The open spaces and gardens provide perfect picnic spots.

Theatre and Music: Check out the Open Air Theatre during the summer months for family-friendly performances. It's a unique way to enjoy theatre in a natural setting.

Personal Story: Our visit to the London Zoo was a highlight of our trip. The kids were thrilled to see the penguin feeding and interact with the animals in the petting zoo. We spent the entire day exploring and learning about different species.

Kew Gardens

Kew Gardens, also known as the Royal Botanic Gardens, is a world-renowned botanical garden with stunning landscapes, historic glasshouses, and a wide variety of plant species. It's a fantastic place for families to explore nature and learn about botany.

Personal Experience: Kew Gardens offered a perfect blend of education and relaxation. The kids were fascinated by the giant tropical plants in the Palm House, and we loved the tranquility of the vast gardens.

Highlights of Kew Gardens

The Palm House: This iconic Victorian glasshouse is home to a diverse collection of tropical plants. Walking through the humid, lush environment felt like stepping into a different world.

The Treetop Walkway: This 18-meter-high walkway offers a bird's-eye view of the gardens. It's an adventurous experience for kids and provides stunning views of the surrounding area.

The Hive: This unique structure mimics a beehive and highlights the importance of bees in our ecosystem. It's both visually striking and educational.

Children's Garden: Designed for ages 2 to 12, this interactive garden encourages kids to explore nature through play. Features include water play areas, sand pits, and giant trees to climb.

Practical Tips

Tickets: Book tickets online in advance to save time and often money. Kew Gardens can be busy, especially on weekends and holidays.

Guided Tours: Consider joining a guided tour to learn more about the history and significance of the gardens. There are also family-friendly tours available.

Pack for the Day: The gardens are extensive, so wear comfortable walking shoes and bring water and snacks. There are several cafes, but having your own provisions can be handy.

Personal Story: The Treetop Walkway was an unforgettable experience. The kids loved being high above the ground, and we enjoyed the panoramic views. It was a highlight of our visit to Kew Gardens.

Final Tips for Visiting Parks and Outdoor Spaces

Engage the Kids: Use interactive maps and activity trails to keep the kids engaged. Many parks offer family-friendly guides and scavenger hunts.

Comfortable Clothing: Wear comfortable clothes and shoes suitable for walking and playing. Bring layers and rain gear as London's weather can be unpredictable.

Stay Hydrated and Snack Smart: Carry water bottles and snacks to keep everyone hydrated and energized. While cafes and kiosks are available, having your own snacks provides flexibility.

Photography: Don't forget your camera or smartphone. These parks offer plenty of picturesque spots and memorable moments to capture.

Entertainment: West End Shows, London Eye, KidZania

London is a city bursting with entertainment options for families. From world-renowned theater productions to breathtaking city views and immersive role-playing experiences, there's something for everyone.

West End Shows

The West End is synonymous with world-class theatre, offering a variety of shows that cater to all ages. Taking your family to a West End show can be a magical and memorable experience.

Personal Experience: Watching a West End show with my family was a highlight of our trip. The kids were mesmerized by the live performances, and it was a fantastic way to introduce them to the arts.

Popular Family-Friendly Shows

The Lion King: This iconic production features stunning visuals, catchy songs, and a heartwarming story that appeals to both kids and adults.

Matilda the Musical: Based on Roald Dahl's beloved book, this show combines humor, brilliant performances, and an inspiring story of a young girl's courage.

Aladdin: With its vibrant costumes, spectacular special effects, and beloved songs, Aladdin is a delightful experience for the whole family.

Practical Tips

Book Tickets in Advance: Popular shows can sell out quickly, so it's best to book your tickets well in advance. Look for family packages or discounts for matinee performances.

Check Age Recommendations: Some shows may have age recommendations or restrictions, so make sure the show is suitable for your children.

Arrive Early: Arriving early ensures you have time to find your seats, buy snacks, and settle in before the show starts. It also gives kids a chance to explore the theatre and soak in the atmosphere.

Personal Story: Our family attended a matinee performance of Matilda the Musical. The kids were captivated by the story and performances, and we all left the theater singing the songs. It was a truly magical afternoon.

London Eye

The London Eye is one of the city's most iconic attractions, offering panoramic views of London from its 135-meter-tall observation wheel. It's a must-visit for families looking to see the city from a unique perspective.

Personal Experience: Our ride on the London Eye was unforgettable. The kids were amazed by the views, and it gave us a fantastic overview of the city's landmarks.

Highlights of the London Eye

Spectacular Views: Each rotation lasts about 30 minutes, providing stunning views of landmarks like Big Ben, the Houses of Parliament, and St. Paul's Cathedral.

Interactive Guides: The capsules are equipped with interactive touchscreens that provide information about the landmarks you see, making it an educational experience as well.

Special Experiences: Consider booking a private capsule or a special experience like the Champagne Experience for a unique treat.

Practical Tips

Book Tickets Online: Purchasing tickets in advance can save you time and often money. The Fast Track tickets are especially useful to skip the long lines.

Best Times to Visit: Early morning or late afternoon tend to be less crowded and offer beautiful lighting for photos.

Prepare for Weather: The capsules are climate-controlled, but it's still a good idea to check the weather forecast. Clear days provide the best views.

Personal Story: We booked a ride on the London Eye for just before sunset. Watching the city lights come on as we rose above the skyline was a breathtaking experience that the whole family enjoyed.

KidZania

KidZania is an indoor city run by kids, offering a unique, interactive learning experience where children can try out different careers in a fun and safe environment.

Personal Experience: Our visit to KidZania was a huge hit with the kids. They loved the freedom to explore different professions and earn "kidZos" (KidZania currency) for their work.

Highlights of KidZania

Role-Playing Activities: Kids can try out over 60 different professions, including being a pilot, firefighter, doctor, or chef. Each activity is designed to be educational and fun.

Earning and Spending KidZos: Children earn kidZos for participating in activities and can spend them on various treats and experiences within KidZania.

Educational Fun: The activities are designed to teach kids about teamwork, financial literacy, and the value of hard work in a fun and engaging way.

Practical Tips

Book in Advance: KidZania is very popular, so it's best to book your tickets online ahead of time. This also allows you to choose your preferred time slot.

Plan Your Visit: Each visit lasts about 4 hours. Make sure to arrive on time to maximize your experience. Review the map and activity list with your kids beforehand to decide which professions they want to try.

Dress Comfortably: Kids will be moving around a lot, so make sure they wear comfortable clothes and shoes.

Personal Story: Our kids spent the entire session at KidZania running from one job to another. They particularly enjoyed being firefighters and putting out a simulated fire. Watching them take on these roles with such enthusiasm was incredibly rewarding.

Combining Your Visit

To make the most of your day, consider combining these entertainment options in a way that suits your family's schedule and interests.

Sample Itinerary

Morning: Start with a visit to KidZania. Spend the morning exploring the different professions and letting the kids earn their kidZos.

Lunch: Have lunch at one of the family-friendly restaurants near KidZania. There are plenty of options to choose from in Westfield London, where KidZania is located.

Afternoon: Head to the London Eye for a relaxing ride and spectacular views of the city. If you time it right, you can catch the sunset for an extra special experience.

Evening: Finish the day with a West End show. Choose a family-friendly performance and enjoy the magic of live theater.

Personal Touch: We found that spacing out these activities with breaks for meals and relaxation helped keep the kids engaged and energized throughout the day.

Final Tips for Family Entertainment

Engage the Kids: Talk to your kids about the activities and get them involved in planning. This makes them more excited and invested in the experiences.

Comfortable Footwear: You'll be on your feet a lot, so wear comfortable shoes to ensure everyone stays happy and comfortable.

Stay Hydrated and Snack Smart: Bring water bottles and snacks to keep everyone hydrated and satisfied, especially if you're on the go.

Photography: Capture the memories with plenty of photos. Whether it's the view from the London Eye or the kids in costume at KidZania, these moments are worth preserving.

Day Trips from London
Harry Potter Studio Tour

For fans of the magical world of Harry Potter, the Warner Bros. Studio Tour London – The Making of Harry Potter is an unmissable experience. Located just outside of London, this immersive tour offers a behind-the-scenes look at the creation of the beloved film series.

Overview of the Tour

The Harry Potter Studio Tour provides a unique opportunity to explore the sets, props, and costumes used in the Harry Potter films. It's a magical journey through the world of Hogwarts, Diagon Alley, and beyond.

Personal Experience: Our family's visit to the Harry Potter Studio Tour was like stepping into the pages of J.K. Rowling's books. The kids were thrilled to see the Great Hall and ride broomsticks, and we all marveled at the intricate details of the sets and props.

Highlights of the Tour

The Great Hall: One of the first sets you'll see is the iconic Great Hall of Hogwarts. Walking through this majestic space, complete with long tables and original costumes, sets the tone for the rest of the tour.

Hogwarts Express and Platform 9 ¾: Climb aboard the Hogwarts Express and pose with your trolley at Platform 9 ¾. This section of the tour is a favorite for photo opportunities.

Diagon Alley: Stroll down the cobbled streets of Diagon Alley and explore the shopfronts of Ollivanders, Weasleys' Wizard Wheezes, and Gringotts Bank.

The Forbidden Forest: Enter the eerie Forbidden Forest and encounter magical creatures like Buckbeak the Hippogriff and Aragog the giant spider.

Gringotts Wizarding Bank: This spectacular set features the impressive marble pillars, goblin tellers, and even a vault filled with treasures.

Practical Tips

Book Tickets in Advance: The Harry Potter Studio Tour is extremely popular, and tickets often sell out months in advance. Book your tickets online as early as possible to secure your preferred date and time slot.

Getting There: The studio is located in Leavesden, just outside of London. You can take a direct train from London Euston to Watford Junction, where a shuttle bus will take you to the studio. Alternatively, there are tour packages that include transportation from central London.

Personal Story: We took the train from London Euston to Watford Junction, and the shuttle bus was easy to find. The kids were excited from the moment we boarded the bus, which was decorated with Harry Potter images.

Plan Your Visit

Duration: The tour is self-guided and typically takes around 3 to 4 hours, but you can easily spend more time if you want to explore everything in detail.

Arrival: Arrive at least 20 minutes before your scheduled entry time to allow for ticket collection and security checks.

Dress Comfortably: Wear comfortable shoes, as there is a lot of walking involved. The tour covers both indoor and outdoor areas, so dress appropriately for the weather.

Interactive Experiences

Green Screen Broomstick Ride: One of the highlights for kids is the chance to ride a broomstick in front of a green screen and see themselves flying over London and Hogwarts.

Butterbeer: Don't miss the opportunity to try Butterbeer at the halfway point of the tour. The kids loved the frothy drink, and we enjoyed the unique taste.

Souvenir Photos: There are several opportunities for souvenir photos, including riding a broomstick or posing in front of iconic sets.

Making the Most of Your Visit

Download the App: The official studio tour app provides additional information, behind-the-scenes facts, and interactive features to enhance your visit. It's a great way to engage the kids and learn more about the making of the films.

Engage with the Exhibits: Encourage the kids to read the information panels and watch the short documentaries throughout the tour. The behind-the-scenes stories add depth to the experience and highlight the creativity and hard work involved in bringing the magical world to life.

Personal Story: Our kids were fascinated by the details of the costume and prop designs. They spent a lot of time in the Creature Effects department, learning about the animatronics and special effects used to create magical creatures.

Dining Options: The Backlot Cafe, located about halfway through the tour, offers a variety of meals and snacks, including themed treats like Butterbeer ice cream. There's also a cafe near the entrance for pre- or post-tour refreshments.

Souvenirs: The gift shop at the end of the tour is filled with Harry Potter merchandise, from wands and robes to chocolate frogs and Bertie Bott's Every Flavor Beans. Set a budget with the kids beforehand to manage expectations.

Personal Story: Each of our kids chose a different souvenir to remember the trip. One picked out a replica of Hermione's wand, while the other opted for a Gryffindor scarf. These items became treasured mementos of our magical day.

Final Tips for Visiting the Harry Potter Studio Tour

Take Your Time: Don't rush through the exhibits. Allow plenty of time to take in the details and enjoy the experience. There's no time limit once you're inside, so make the most of it.

Photography: Photography is allowed throughout most of the tour, so bring your camera or smartphone to capture the memories. Some areas, like the green screen experiences, may have specific restrictions, so be sure to check the guidelines.

Engage the Kids: Use the interactive elements and behind-the-scenes stories to keep the kids engaged and excited. Encourage them to ask questions and explore at their own pace.

Comfortable Footwear: With lots of walking and standing, comfortable shoes are essential. The tour covers a significant area, and you'll want to be comfortable throughout.

Stay Hydrated: Carry water bottles, especially during warmer weather. There are cafes and vending machines throughout the tour, but having your own water is convenient.

Windsor Castle

Windsor Castle, the oldest and largest occupied castle in the world, is a must-visit for anyone interested in British history and royalty. Located just outside of London, this magnificent castle has been a royal residence for over 900 years.

Overview of Windsor Castle

Windsor Castle is not only a historical monument but also an active royal residence, often used by the Queen for state occasions and ceremonies. The castle offers a rich blend of history, architecture, and art, making it a fascinating destination for families.

Highlights of Windsor Castle

State Apartments: These rooms are lavishly decorated with some of the finest works of art from the Royal Collection, including paintings by Rembrandt and

Rubens. The kids were particularly impressed by the opulent furnishings and the grandeur of the rooms.

St. George's Chapel: This beautiful Gothic chapel is the burial site of many monarchs, including Henry VIII and Charles I. It's also where Prince Harry and Meghan Markle were married. The intricate architecture and historic significance make it a must-see.

Queen Mary's Dolls' House: This miniature royal residence is a marvel of craftsmanship. It's furnished with tiny, exquisitely detailed items, including working electricity and running water. The kids were fascinated by the tiny details and the grandeur in miniature.

Changing of the Guard: Witnessing this iconic ceremony at Windsor Castle is a unique experience. The precision and pageantry of the guards are captivating, especially for younger visitors.

Practical Tips

Book Tickets in Advance: Windsor Castle is a popular attraction, and booking tickets online in advance is recommended. This can save you time and often includes a timed entry slot to manage crowds.

Getting There: Windsor is easily accessible from London. You can take a direct train from London Paddington to Windsor & Eton Central, or from London Waterloo to Windsor & Eton Riverside. The journey takes about an hour, and the castle is a short walk from either station.

Personal Story: We took the train from London Paddington to Windsor & Eton Central. The journey was comfortable, and the short walk to the castle through the charming town of Windsor added to the experience.

Plan Your Visit

Arrival: Arrive early to make the most of your day. The castle opens at 10:00 AM, and getting there early helps you avoid the busiest times.

Audio Guides: Take advantage of the free audio guides available at the entrance. They provide detailed information about each part of the castle and help engage kids with interesting stories and facts.

Comfortable Footwear: There's a lot of walking involved, both inside the castle and around the grounds, so wear comfortable shoes.

Interactive Experiences

Family Trails: Pick up a family trail at the entrance to keep the kids engaged. These trails guide you through the castle with fun facts and activities designed for younger visitors.

Photo Opportunities: There are plenty of great spots for family photos, including the impressive entrance gate, the stunning views from the North Terrace, and the beautiful gardens.

Making the Most of Your Visit

St. George's Chapel: Plan your visit to the chapel around the times of the services to avoid interruptions. The chapel is an active place of worship, so some areas might be restricted during services.

Changing of the Guard: Check the schedule for the Changing of the Guard ceremony. It usually takes place on select days and is a popular event, so arrive early to secure a good viewing spot.

Dining Options: There are several cafes and restaurants within Windsor town, offering a variety of dining options. For a special treat, consider having afternoon tea at one of the traditional tea rooms.

Personal Story: We enjoyed a delightful afternoon tea at a local tea room after our visit. It was a perfect way to relax and reflect on our day at the castle.

Exploring Windsor: After your visit to the castle, take some time to explore the town of Windsor. The picturesque streets are lined with shops, cafes, and historic buildings, offering a charming setting for a leisurely stroll.

Souvenirs: The castle's gift shop offers a range of souvenirs, from royal-themed gifts to local crafts. Set a budget with the kids beforehand to manage expectations.

Final Tips for Visiting Windsor Castle

Engage the Kids: Use the audio guides and family trails to keep the kids interested and engaged. Encourage them to ask questions and explore at their own pace.

Photography: Bring a camera or smartphone to capture the memories. While photography is not allowed inside the State Apartments, there are plenty of picturesque spots around the castle and grounds.

Comfortable Clothing: Dress in layers and bring rain gear if the weather is uncertain. The castle grounds are extensive, and you'll spend a good amount of time outdoors.

Stay Hydrated and Snack Smart: Carry water bottles and snacks to keep everyone hydrated and satisfied throughout the day. While there are cafes, having your own provisions can be convenient, especially with younger children.

Legoland Windsor

Legoland Windsor is one of the UK's most popular family attractions, offering a magical world of LEGO-themed rides, shows, and interactive experiences. Located just a short distance from Windsor, it's a perfect day trip for families visiting London or the surrounding areas.

Overview of Legoland Windsor

Legoland Windsor is a theme park designed especially for families with children aged 2 to 12. The park is divided into themed areas, each offering a variety of rides, attractions, and interactive experiences that bring the world of LEGO to life.

Highlights of Legoland Windsor

Miniland: A must-see area featuring incredibly detailed miniature versions of famous landmarks from around the world, all made from millions of LEGO bricks. The kids loved spotting familiar buildings and seeing the moving trains and boats.

LEGO Ninjago World: This area includes the Ninjago Ride, an interactive 4D experience where you use hand gestures to fight off virtual enemies. It was a favorite for our kids, who are big fans of the Ninjago series.

Duplo Valley: Perfect for younger children, this area includes gentle rides, water play areas, and a splash zone. The Duplo Train and Duplo Dino Coaster are great fun for little ones.

Pirate Shores: Featuring water-based rides and pirate-themed attractions, this area is perfect for adventurous kids. The Pirate Falls Treasure Quest was a hit with our family, offering a mix of excitement and splashes.

LEGO City: This section includes driving schools where kids can get their own "driving license," a fire academy, and the Coastguard HQ boat ride. The driving school was particularly popular with our kids.

Practical Tips

Book Tickets in Advance: Legoland Windsor is very popular, and booking tickets online in advance is highly recommended. This can save you money and guarantee entry, especially during peak times.

Getting There: Legoland Windsor is located about 25 miles from central London. You can take a direct train from London Paddington to Windsor & Eton Central, then a short bus or taxi ride to the park. Alternatively, there are direct shuttle buses from central London to Legoland.

Personal Story: We took the train from London Paddington and then a shuttle bus from Windsor to Legoland. The journey was smooth, and the kids were excited from the moment we boarded the LEGO-themed shuttle bus.

Plan Your Visit

Arrival: Arrive early to make the most of your day. The park opens at 10:00 AM, and getting there when it opens helps you beat the crowds and enjoy popular rides with shorter wait times.

Height Restrictions: Check the height requirements for rides in advance to avoid disappointment. Many rides have minimum height requirements, but there are plenty of attractions for all ages.

Stroller Rentals: If you have younger children, consider renting a stroller at the park. It's a large area, and little legs can get tired.

Interactive Experiences

LEGO Building Workshops: Participate in LEGO building workshops where kids can learn new building techniques and create their own LEGO masterpieces.

Character Meet and Greets: Don't miss the chance to meet LEGO characters like Emmet and Wyldstyle from The LEGO Movie. Check the schedule for character appearances.

Dining Options

Picnic Areas: Legoland has designated picnic areas if you prefer to bring your own food. This can be a great way to save money and ensure you have familiar snacks for picky eaters.

Restaurants and Cafes: There are several dining options within the park, including pizza, burgers, and healthier choices like salads and wraps. We enjoyed a meal at Pirate's Burger Kitchen, which offered a good variety and kid-friendly options.

Personal Story: We packed a picnic for our visit and found a lovely spot in the park to enjoy our lunch. It was a nice break from the rides and allowed us to relax and recharge before continuing our adventure.

Making the Most of Your Visit

Plan Your Route: The park is large, so plan your route to make the most of your time. Prioritize the areas and rides that are most important to your family, and use the park map to navigate efficiently.

Queue Management: Use the Reserve & Ride system (formerly known as Q-Bot) to reduce wait times for popular rides. This system allows you to reserve a spot in line and return when it's your turn, giving you more time to explore other attractions.

Personal Story: We used the Reserve & Ride system for the most popular rides, which significantly reduced our wait times and made the day much more enjoyable.

Stay Hydrated and Snack Smart: Bring water bottles and snacks to keep everyone hydrated and energized throughout the day. There are water refill stations throughout the park.

Souvenirs: The park's gift shops offer a wide range of LEGO sets, themed merchandise, and souvenirs. Set a budget with the kids beforehand to manage expectations.

Final Tips for Visiting Legoland Windsor

Engage the Kids: Use the interactive elements and hands-on activities to keep the kids engaged and excited. Encourage them to explore and participate in building workshops and interactive rides.

Comfortable Clothing: Dress in comfortable clothes and shoes suitable for walking and playing. Bring a change of clothes or swimwear for the water play areas.

Photography: Capture the memories with plenty of photos. The park's colorful and imaginative settings provide fantastic photo opportunities.

Stay for the Shows: Legoland offers a variety of live shows and entertainment throughout the day. Check the schedule and make time to enjoy a show or two for a break from the rides.

Brighton Beach

Brighton Beach, located on the southern coast of England, is a popular seaside destination known for its vibrant atmosphere, historic pier, and pebbly shores. Just a short train ride from London, Brighton offers a perfect day trip or weekend getaway for families.

Overview of Brighton Beach

Brighton Beach is famous for its lively seafront, charming lanes, and eclectic mix of attractions. The city's blend of traditional seaside fun and modern amenities makes it an ideal spot for families.

Highlights of Brighton Beach

Brighton Pier: The iconic Brighton Pier is packed with rides, arcade games, and food stalls. It's a must-visit for families looking for some classic seaside entertainment.

The Beach: Unlike sandy beaches, Brighton Beach is pebbly, which can be a fun novelty for kids. The clear water and fresh sea air make it a great spot for a paddle or a picnic.

The Lanes: A maze of narrow, winding streets filled with unique shops, cafes, and boutiques. It's a great place to explore and find some interesting souvenirs.

British Airways i360: This observation tower offers stunning 360-degree views of Brighton and the surrounding coastline. The kids were thrilled by the gentle ascent and the panoramic vistas.

Practical Tips

Getting There: Brighton is easily accessible from London. You can take a direct train from London Victoria or London Bridge to Brighton Station.

The journey takes about an hour, and from the station, it's a short walk to the beach and main attractions.

Personal Story: We took the train from London Victoria and enjoyed the scenic journey through the English countryside. The kids were excited as soon as we arrived at Brighton Station, with the beach just a short walk away.

Plan Your Visit

Weather: Check the weather forecast before your trip. Brighton can be windy, and it's best to dress in layers and bring a windbreaker or light jacket.

Comfortable Footwear: The beach is pebbly, so wearing sturdy shoes or sandals is more comfortable than barefoot. Bring water shoes if you plan to paddle in the sea.

Sun Protection: On sunny days, ensure everyone has sunscreen, hats, and sunglasses to protect against the sun's rays.

Interactive Experiences

Rides and Games: Brighton Pier offers a variety of rides and arcade games. From traditional carousel rides to thrilling roller coasters, there's something for every age group.

Beach Activities: Bring a beach ball, Frisbee, or kite for some family fun on the beach. The kids enjoyed skipping stones and collecting unique pebbles as keepsakes.

Sea Life Brighton: Visit the Sea Life Brighton aquarium, located near the beach. It's the world's oldest operating aquarium and features a wide range of marine life, including sharks, turtles, and rays.

Dining Options

Seafront Cafes: Brighton's seafront is lined with cafes and food stalls offering everything from traditional fish and chips to international cuisine. We enjoyed a tasty lunch at a beachside cafe, complete with stunning sea views.

Picnic on the Beach: Pack a picnic and find a spot on the beach to enjoy your meal. The fresh sea air and the sound of the waves make for a relaxing and enjoyable dining experience.

Personal Story: We packed a picnic and found a cozy spot on the beach. The kids loved eating their sandwiches while watching the waves, and we all enjoyed the laid-back seaside vibe.

Making the Most of Your Visit

Explore The Lanes: After some beach time, take a stroll through The Lanes. The narrow streets are filled with unique shops, street performers, and quaint cafes. It's a great place to wander and discover hidden gems.

Ride the British Airways i360: For breathtaking views of Brighton and the coast, take a ride on the British Airways i360. The glass observation pod slowly ascends to 450 feet, offering stunning panoramic views. The kids were fascinated by the gentle ascent and the incredible vistas.

Personal Story: Our ride on the i360 was a highlight of the day. The kids were amazed by the views, and we all enjoyed spotting landmarks and taking photos from the top.

Beachfront Playgrounds: Brighton Beach has several playgrounds along the seafront, perfect for letting the kids burn off some energy. These well-maintained play areas offer a variety of equipment and are great for younger children.

Cultural Attractions: Brighton is home to several museums and cultural attractions, including the Brighton Museum & Art Gallery and the Royal Pavilion, a former royal residence with stunning architecture and beautiful gardens.

Personal Story: We visited the Royal Pavilion and were captivated by its exotic architecture and opulent interiors. The kids enjoyed exploring the gardens and learning about the history of the building.

Final Tips for Visiting Brighton Beach

Engage the Kids: Use interactive elements and activities to keep the kids engaged and excited. Encourage them to explore the beach, play games, and participate in the rides and attractions.

Comfortable Clothing: Dress in comfortable clothes suitable for beach activities and walking. Bring a change of clothes if the kids plan to paddle or play in the water.

Photography: Capture the memories with plenty of photos. The vibrant seafront, iconic pier, and picturesque Lanes provide fantastic photo opportunities.

Stay Hydrated and Snack Smart: Bring water bottles and snacks to keep everyone hydrated and satisfied throughout the day. While there are plenty of food options, having your own provisions can be convenient.

Eating Out with Kids
Family-Friendly Restaurants

London is home to a diverse culinary scene, offering a wide range of family-friendly restaurants that cater to all tastes and preferences. Whether you're looking for a casual dining experience, a place with interactive activities for kids, or a restaurant with a unique theme, London has plenty of options to keep everyone happy.

Rainforest Cafe

Located near Piccadilly Circus, the Rainforest Cafe offers a unique dining experience set in a lush, jungle-themed environment complete with animatronic animals, cascading waterfalls, and tropical thunderstorms.

Highlights

Themed Decor: The rainforest theme is brought to life with vibrant decor, animatronic animals, and sound effects. The kids loved the periodic "thunderstorms" and watching the animated gorillas and elephants.

Kid-Friendly Menu: The menu features a variety of dishes, including burgers, pasta, and salads, with a dedicated kids' menu offering favorites like chicken tenders and mac and cheese.

Interactive Experience: The restaurant shop sells rainforest-themed toys and souvenirs, adding an extra layer of excitement for the kids.

Practical Tips

Reservations: The Rainforest Cafe is popular, especially on weekends and holidays. Make a reservation in advance to ensure a table.

Allow Extra Time: Plan to spend some extra time exploring the decor and visiting the gift shop.

Pizza Express

With multiple locations across London, Pizza Express is a reliable and family-friendly option offering delicious pizzas, pastas, and salads in a relaxed setting.

Highlights

Kids' Menu: The Piccolo menu is designed for children and includes a starter, main course, dessert, and drink. The DIY pizza kit lets kids create their own pizza, which they love.

Family-Friendly Atmosphere: The relaxed and casual setting makes it easy for families to enjoy a meal together without feeling rushed.

Quality Food: The menu offers a variety of pizzas, pastas, and salads made with fresh ingredients. There are also gluten-free and vegetarian options available.

Practical Tips

Reservations: While it's usually easy to get a table, making a reservation can save time, especially during peak dining hours.

Look for Deals: Pizza Express often has special offers and discounts, so check their website or app for the latest deals.

Dishoom

Dishoom offers a taste of Bombay in London, with several locations throughout the city. Known for its delicious Indian cuisine and vibrant atmosphere, it's a great option for families looking to try something different.

Personal Experience: Our meal at Dishoom was a culinary adventure. The kids enjoyed trying new flavors, and the lively atmosphere made it a fun dining experience for the whole family.

Highlights

Delicious Food: The menu features a range of Indian dishes, from traditional curries to street food-inspired snacks. The kids' menu includes milder options that are still full of flavor.

Welcoming Atmosphere: The decor and ambiance are inspired by old Bombay cafes, creating a warm and inviting setting. The staff are friendly and accommodating to families.

Breakfast and Brunch: Dishoom is also known for its delicious breakfast and brunch options, including bacon naan rolls and spiced eggs.

Practical Tips

Reservations: Dishoom is very popular, and reservations are recommended, especially for dinner. Walk-ins are also welcome, but expect a wait during peak times.

Family Style Dining: Order a variety of dishes to share, allowing everyone to try different flavors and find their favorites.

The Diner

The Diner, with multiple locations across London, offers an American-style dining experience with a fun and relaxed atmosphere. It's perfect for families craving classic American comfort food.

Highlights

American Comfort Food: The menu includes burgers, hot dogs, pancakes, and milkshakes. The kids' menu features smaller portions of popular dishes.

Retro Decor: The 1950s diner theme, complete with red booths and jukeboxes, creates a fun and nostalgic atmosphere.

Milkshakes: The Diner is known for its delicious milkshakes, which come in a variety of flavors and can be customized with different toppings.

Practical Tips

Reservations: The Diner can get busy, especially on weekends. Making a reservation is recommended to avoid waiting.

Special Offers: Check their website for special offers and kids-eat-free promotions.

Giraffe

Giraffe is a family-friendly chain with several locations across London, offering a diverse menu inspired by global flavors. It's a great choice for families looking for a casual dining experience.

Personal Experience: Giraffe was a hit with our family due to its varied menu and relaxed atmosphere. The kids loved the playful decor and trying dishes from different cuisines.

Highlights

Global Menu: The menu features a mix of dishes from around the world, including tacos, stir-fries, burgers, and salads. The kids' menu offers a variety of options, from pasta to fish fingers.

Kid-Friendly Atmosphere: The bright and colorful decor, along with friendly staff, make it a welcoming place for families.

Brunch: Giraffe also offers a great brunch menu, with options like avocado toast, pancakes, and full English breakfasts.

Practical Tips

Reservations: While Giraffe is usually able to accommodate walk-ins, making a reservation can ensure you get a table at your preferred time.

Kids' Activities: Some locations offer coloring sheets and crayons to keep the kids entertained while waiting for their food.

Final Tips for Dining Out with Family

Engage the Kids: Look for restaurants that offer activities or interactive elements, like make-your-own pizza kits or coloring sheets. This keeps the kids entertained and engaged.

Comfortable Environment: Choose places with a relaxed and casual atmosphere where kids can be kids without the pressure of formal dining.

Healthy Options: Many family-friendly restaurants offer healthy menu options, including vegetarian, gluten-free, and dairy-free choices. This ensures everyone in the family can find something they enjoy.

Plan Ahead: Make reservations when possible, especially for popular restaurants and during peak dining times. This helps avoid long waits and ensures a smoother dining experience.

Stay Hydrated and Snack Smart: Bring water bottles and small snacks to keep the kids hydrated and satisfied, especially if there's a wait for your table or food.

Dining out in London with your family can be a delightful experience with the right choice of restaurants. These family-friendly options offer delicious food, engaging atmospheres, and activities to keep the kids entertained.

Cafes and Bakeries

London's vibrant culinary scene includes a delightful array of cafes and bakeries, perfect for family outings. Whether you're looking for a cozy spot for breakfast, a mid-day treat, or a relaxed afternoon tea, the city offers plenty of options to satisfy everyone's cravings.

Here's a detailed guide to some of the best family-friendly cafes and bakeries in London.

Peggy Porschen

Located in Belgravia, Peggy Porschen is a picture-perfect bakery known for its beautifully decorated cakes and pastel-hued decor. It's a fantastic spot for a sweet treat and a dose of Instagram-worthy charm.

Highlights

Cakes and Pastries: The menu features an array of cupcakes, layer cakes, cookies, and other sweet treats, all beautifully decorated and delicious.

Tea and Coffee: Enjoy a cup of tea, coffee, or hot chocolate to accompany your treats. The kids loved the indulgent hot chocolate topped with whipped cream.

Instagram-Worthy Decor: The pink exterior and floral displays make Peggy Porschen one of the most photographed cafes in London. The kids enjoyed posing for photos with their colorful cupcakes.

Practical Tips

Seating: Peggy Porschen can get busy, especially on weekends. Arriving early or visiting on a weekday can help you secure a table.

Special Occasions: The bakery also offers custom cakes for special occasions. Consider ordering a cake for a birthday or celebration.

The Breakfast Club

With several locations across London, The Breakfast Club is known for its hearty breakfasts and fun, retro vibe. It's a great spot for a family breakfast or brunch.

Highlights

Hearty Breakfasts: The menu features classic breakfast dishes like pancakes, French toast, eggs Benedict, and full English breakfasts. The kids' menu includes smaller portions of these favorites.

Retro Decor: Each location has a unique, retro-inspired decor that adds to the fun and welcoming atmosphere.

Friendly Staff: The staff are friendly and accommodating, making it a comfortable place for families with young children.

Practical Tips

Reservations: The Breakfast Club locations can get busy, especially on weekends. While they don't take reservations for small groups, arriving early can help you avoid long waits.

All-Day Menu: The menu is available all day, so you can enjoy breakfast for lunch or dinner if you prefer.

Gail's Bakery

Gail's Bakery, with multiple locations throughout London, offers a wonderful selection of freshly baked bread, pastries, and cakes. It's a great spot for a casual breakfast, lunch, or a snack.

Highlights

Freshly Baked Goods: Gail's is known for its high-quality bread, croissants, cakes, and pastries. The kids particularly loved the chocolate croissants and cinnamon buns.

Healthy Options: In addition to sweet treats, Gail's offers a range of healthy options, including salads, sandwiches, and soups.

Comfortable Seating: The relaxed atmosphere and comfortable seating make it a great spot to unwind and enjoy a meal with the family.

Practical Tips

Grab-and-Go: If you're on the go, Gail's is perfect for grabbing a quick coffee and pastry to take with you.

Allergy-Friendly: Gail's offers several gluten-free and dairy-free options. Ask the staff about their allergy-friendly choices.

Ben's Cookies

For a sweet treat, Ben's Cookies is a must-visit. Known for their delicious, freshly baked cookies, this bakery has several locations across London.

Highlights

Delicious Cookies: The menu features a wide range of cookie flavors, including classics like chocolate chip, oatmeal raisin, and white chocolate macadamia. The cookies are baked fresh throughout the day.

Takeaway Treats: Ben's Cookies are perfect for a quick snack or a takeaway treat to enjoy later.

Gift Tins: The bakery also offers gift tins, which make great souvenirs or gifts for friends and family.

Practical Tips

Flavor Variety: Try a variety of flavors to find your favorites. The kids loved sampling different types and choosing their top picks.

Freshness: The cookies are best enjoyed fresh, so eat them soon after purchase for the ultimate gooey experience.

Cutter & Squidge

Located in Soho, Cutter & Squidge is a charming bakery and cafe known for its imaginative cakes, biskies (a cross between a biscuit, cake, and cookie), and afternoon tea.

Highlights

Afternoon Tea: The afternoon tea includes a selection of finger sandwiches, scones, pastries, and their signature biskies. It's a delightful experience for both kids and adults.

Unique Treats: In addition to traditional baked goods, Cutter & Squidge offers unique creations like their famous biskies and dream cakes.

Themed Experiences: The bakery often hosts themed afternoon teas, such as the Wizarding Afternoon Tea, inspired by Harry Potter. These experiences add an extra layer of fun and magic.

Practical Tips

Reservations: Afternoon tea at Cutter & Squidge is popular, so it's best to make a reservation in advance.

Themed Events: Check their website for themed afternoon teas and special events. These can be a fun way to add a bit of magic to your visit.

Final Tips for Family-Friendly Cafes and Bakeries

Engage the Kids: Look for cafes and bakeries that offer interactive elements or special treats for kids. Choosing their own pastries or participating in themed events can make the experience more enjoyable.

Comfortable Seating: Choose places with comfortable seating and a relaxed atmosphere where kids can feel at ease.

Healthy Options: Many cafes and bakeries offer healthy menu options, including gluten-free and dairy-free choices. This ensures that everyone in the family can find something they enjoy.

Plan Ahead: Make reservations when possible, especially for popular spots and themed events. This helps avoid long waits and ensures a smoother dining experience.

Stay Hydrated and Snack Smart: Bring water bottles and small snacks to keep the kids hydrated and satisfied, especially if you're on the go.

Picnicking Spots

London boasts a wealth of beautiful parks and green spaces, perfect for family picnics. Whether you're looking for a spot with playgrounds for the kids, scenic views, or tranquil settings, the city has something to offer.

Hyde Park

Hyde Park is one of London's largest and most famous parks, offering a variety of activities and picturesque spots for a family picnic.

Highlights

The Serpentine: Find a spot by the Serpentine Lake for a scenic picnic with views of swans and boats. After your meal, you can rent a pedal boat or take a leisurely stroll along the lake.

Diana Memorial Playground: Located in the northwest corner of the park, this Peter Pan-themed playground is a fantastic spot for kids to play. It's enclosed and features a pirate ship, teepees, and various play structures.

Open Lawns: Hyde Park has plenty of open grassy areas perfect for spreading out a blanket and enjoying a picnic. The wide lawns offer ample space for kids to run and play.

Practical Tips

Arrive Early: Hyde Park can get busy, especially on weekends and sunny days. Arriving early ensures you find a good spot.

Facilities: The park has several restrooms and cafes if you need additional refreshments or a restroom break.

Regent's Park

Regent's Park is another great choice for a family picnic, with its beautifully landscaped gardens, playgrounds, and open spaces.

Highlights

Queen Mary's Gardens: This stunning rose garden is a peaceful spot for a picnic. The vibrant flowers and well-maintained lawns provide a picturesque backdrop.

Regent's Park Boating Lake: Enjoy a picnic by the lake and watch the rowboats and pedal boats. Afterward, you can rent a boat for a fun family activity.

Playgrounds: The park has several playgrounds, including the Gloucester Gate Playground and the Hanover Gate Playground, which offer a range of equipment for children of all ages.

Practical Tips

Check for Events: Regent's Park hosts various events and open-air theater performances, which can add an extra layer of entertainment to your visit. Check the schedule in advance.

Picnic Areas: The park has designated picnic areas with tables and benches, but you can also spread out a blanket on the grass.

Hampstead Heath

Hampstead Heath offers a more rugged and natural setting, perfect for a family picnic with plenty of space to explore and play.

Highlights

Parliament Hill: This spot offers one of the best views of the London skyline. It's a great place to spread out a blanket and enjoy a picnic while taking in the scenery.

Swimming Ponds: Hampstead Heath has several swimming ponds where you can take a refreshing dip. The mixed pond is family-friendly and a unique addition to your picnic outing.

Woodlands and Fields: The Heath's varied landscape includes woodlands, fields, and meadows, providing plenty of space for kids to run and explore.

Practical Tips

Pack for Adventure: Bring sturdy shoes and be prepared for a bit of hiking if you plan to explore the more rugged areas of the Heath.

Check the Weather: Hampstead Heath is very exposed, so check the weather forecast and dress accordingly. Bring layers and a windbreaker if needed.

Greenwich Park

Greenwich Park is a historic and beautifully landscaped park offering stunning views, playgrounds, and plenty of green space for picnics.

Highlights

The Hill: Find a spot on the hill for a picnic with fantastic views over the River Thames and the city skyline. The view is especially beautiful at sunset.

Children's Playground: The playground near the north entrance of the park offers a variety of equipment for children to enjoy.

The Observatory and Meridian Line: After your picnic, visit the Royal Observatory and stand on the Prime Meridian, where you can learn about the history of navigation and timekeeping.

Practical Tips

Explore the Town: Greenwich is a charming area with markets, shops, and the historic Cutty Sark ship. Consider spending some time exploring the town before or after your picnic.

Facilities: The park has several restrooms and cafes if you need additional amenities.

Victoria Park

Victoria Park, located in East London, is a spacious park with beautiful lakes, playgrounds, and plenty of picnic spots.

Highlights

Boating Lake: Rent a pedal boat or rowboat for a fun activity on the lake. There are also plenty of spots around the lake for a relaxing picnic.

Playgrounds: The park has several well-equipped playgrounds, including the popular Victoria Park Playground, which features a large sandpit, climbing structures, and swings.

Cafes: The park has several cafes offering a range of food and drinks, perfect for picking up a treat or supplementing your picnic.

Practical Tips

Bike Rentals: The park has bike rental stations, making it easy to explore the extensive paths and trails. Consider renting bikes for a family ride around the park.

Events: Check the park's schedule for events like outdoor cinema screenings, markets, and festivals that might coincide with your visit.

Final Tips for Family Picnics

Engage the Kids: Bring along games, balls, or kites to keep the kids entertained. Many parks have open spaces perfect for playing and running around.

Comfortable Seating: Bring a comfortable blanket or folding chairs for your picnic. Consider packing a picnic basket with all the essentials, including napkins, utensils, and a trash bag for clean-up.

Healthy Options: Pack a variety of healthy snacks and drinks to keep everyone satisfied and hydrated. Fresh fruit, sandwiches, and snacks like nuts and cheese are great options.

Check the Weather: Always check the weather forecast before heading out. Bring layers and be prepared for changes in weather, especially in spring and fall.

Stay Hydrated and Snack Smart: Bring plenty of water and healthy snacks to keep everyone hydrated and energized throughout the day.

Special Dietary Needs

London is a diverse and inclusive city that caters to a wide range of dietary needs. Whether you have allergies, follow a vegetarian or vegan diet, or need gluten-free options, you'll find plenty of restaurants, cafes, and bakeries that can accommodate your requirements.

Gluten-Free Options

For those who need to avoid gluten, London offers a variety of restaurants and cafes with gluten-free menus or options.

Personal Experience: Our family has found many excellent gluten-free options in London. The variety and quality of food available make dining out enjoyable and stress-free.

Recommended Places

Niche: Located in Islington, Niche is a 100% gluten-free restaurant offering a delicious menu of British comfort food. From fish and chips to burgers and pasta, everything is gluten-free.

Beyond Bread: This bakery and cafe in Fitzrovia specializes in gluten-free baked goods. Enjoy fresh bread, pastries, and cakes without worrying about gluten.

Dishoom: With several locations across London, Dishoom offers a dedicated gluten-free menu featuring their popular Indian dishes. The friendly staff are knowledgeable about dietary needs.

Practical Tips

Research and Reservations: Research restaurants ahead of time and make reservations if possible. Mention your dietary needs when booking to ensure they can accommodate you.

Gluten-Free Apps: Use apps like Find Me Gluten Free to discover more gluten-free dining options and read reviews from other diners.

Vegetarian and Vegan Options

London is a haven for vegetarians and vegans, with numerous restaurants offering plant-based menus or options.

Personal Experience: As vegetarians, we've always been impressed by the variety and creativity of vegetarian and vegan dishes available in London. From casual cafes to fine dining, there's something for everyone.

Recommended Places

Mildreds: With multiple locations, Mildreds is a popular spot for vegetarian and vegan cuisine. The menu features globally inspired dishes, including burgers, curries, and salads.

Farmacy: Located in Notting Hill, Farmacy offers a plant-based menu focusing on organic and seasonal ingredients. The vibrant dishes and cozy atmosphere make it a great choice for a family meal.

Temple of Seitan: This vegan fast-food joint serves delicious plant-based versions of fried chicken, burgers, and other comfort foods. The kids loved the crispy "chicken" and fries.

Practical Tips

Ask for Recommendations: Don't hesitate to ask the staff for their recommendations or if they can modify dishes to suit your preferences. Many restaurants are happy to accommodate dietary needs.

Explore Markets: London's food markets, like Borough Market and Camden Market, offer a variety of vegetarian and vegan options. It's a great way to sample different cuisines and find unique dishes.

Nut-Free and Allergy-Friendly Options

Dining out with nut allergies or other food allergies can be challenging, but many London restaurants are equipped to handle such dietary needs with care.

Recommended Places

Leon: This chain of fast-food restaurants offers a variety of allergy-friendly options. Their menu clearly labels dishes that are free from common allergens, making it easy to choose safe options.

The Gate: With locations in Islington, Hammersmith, and Marylebone, The Gate offers innovative vegetarian and vegan cuisine. They are very accommodating of allergies and can modify dishes to meet your needs.

By Chloe: Located in Covent Garden, By Chloe is a vegan restaurant that clearly labels its menu for common allergens, including nuts. The staff are knowledgeable and can help you choose safe options.

Practical Tips

Communicate Clearly: Always communicate your allergies clearly to the staff when ordering. Ask about cross-contamination and how they handle food allergies in the kitchen.

Carry Emergency Medication: If you have severe allergies, always carry your emergency medication (like an EpiPen) with you and inform your dining companions about your allergy action plan.

Lactose-Free and Dairy-Free Options

For those who are lactose intolerant or follow a dairy-free diet, London offers many options to ensure you can enjoy delicious meals without discomfort.

Recommended Places

The Vurger Co.: This vegan fast-food restaurant offers delicious plant-based burgers and sides, all free from dairy. It's a hit with kids and adults alike.

Manna: Located in Primrose Hill, Manna is one of London's oldest vegetarian restaurants. Their menu includes a variety of dairy-free options, from appetizers to desserts.

Amorino Gelato: For a sweet treat, Amorino offers a range of dairy-free sorbets that are just as delicious as their traditional gelato. The kids loved the fruity flavors.

Practical Tips

Check Menus Online: Many restaurants post their menus online, including information about dietary options. This can help you plan your meals and avoid surprises.

Ask for Substitutions: Don't hesitate to ask if a dish can be made dairy-free. Many places offer alternative milk options and can modify recipes to accommodate your needs.

Final Tips for Dining with Special Dietary Needs

Research and Plan Ahead: Research restaurants and cafes before your trip to find those that cater to your dietary needs. Make a list of options near your accommodation and popular attractions.

Communicate Clearly: When dining out, clearly communicate your dietary needs to the staff. Ask questions about ingredients, preparation methods, and potential cross-contamination.

Use Apps and Online Resources: Utilize apps and websites dedicated to special dietary needs. They can help you find suitable dining options, read reviews, and get recommendations from other diners with similar needs.

Carry Snacks: It's always a good idea to carry some safe snacks with you, especially if you're exploring new areas or unsure about dining options. This ensures you have something to eat in case of delays or limited choices.

Be Prepared: If you have severe allergies or medical dietary restrictions, carry any necessary medication and have a plan in place for emergencies. Inform your dining companions and restaurant staff about your needs.

Fun and Free Activities

London is a treasure trove of fun and free activities, offering something for everyone. From world-class museums and galleries to beautiful parks and playgrounds, there's no shortage of things to do that won't cost you a penny.

Here's a detailed guide to some of the best free activities in London, including museums, parks, walking tours, and seasonal events.

Free Museums and Galleries

London is home to some of the world's finest museums and galleries, many of which offer free entry. These cultural institutions provide an enriching experience for visitors of all ages.

British Museum

Explore ancient artifacts from around the world, including the Rosetta Stone, the Elgin Marbles, and the Egyptian mummies. The museum offers family-friendly trails and activity packs to keep kids engaged.

Practical Tips: Admission is free, but special exhibitions may require a ticket. Arrive early to avoid crowds, especially during weekends and holidays.

Natural History Museum

Discover the wonders of the natural world, from dinosaur skeletons to precious gems. The Blue Whale skeleton in the Hintze Hall is a must-see.

Practical Tips: Entry is free, but certain temporary exhibits may have an admission fee. The museum is very popular, so consider visiting during weekdays or off-peak hours.

Science Museum

Engage with interactive exhibits on space, technology, and science. The Wonderlab gallery is especially fun for kids, although it requires a paid ticket.

Practical Tips: The main museum is free, but some special exhibitions and the Wonderlab have entry fees. Plan your visit to include the hands-on interactive galleries that are free.

Tate Modern

This contemporary art gallery housed in a former power station offers stunning views of the River Thames and features works by artists like Picasso, Warhol, and Hockney.

Practical Tips: Admission to the main collections is free, but special exhibitions may require a ticket. Don't miss the viewing level for great city views.

National Gallery

Home to a vast collection of European paintings, including works by Van Gogh, Rembrandt, and Da Vinci. The gallery offers family trails and workshops.

Practical Tips: Entry is free, and there are free guided tours and talks available. Pick up a family activity trail at the information desk to engage the kids.

Parks and Playgrounds

London's parks are perfect for a family day out, offering plenty of space to relax, play, and explore.

Hyde Park

Enjoy boating on the Serpentine, visiting the Diana Memorial Playground, and exploring the open lawns and gardens.

Practical Tips: The park is open year-round and has several cafes and restrooms. Bring a picnic and spend the day enjoying the various attractions.

Regent's Park

Features beautiful gardens, a boating lake, playgrounds, and an open-air theater. Queen Mary's Gardens is particularly stunning.

Practical Tips: The park is home to several playgrounds and has plenty of spots for picnicking. Check the schedule for free events and performances.

Greenwich Park

Offers panoramic views of London, playgrounds, and the chance to stand on the Prime Meridian at the Royal Observatory.

Practical Tips: The park is large, so plan your visit to include the main attractions. The nearby Greenwich Market is great for a wander and a snack.

Hampstead Heath

A wilder, more rugged park with woodlands, open fields, and swimming ponds. The views from Parliament Hill are spectacular.

Practical Tips: Wear comfortable shoes and be prepared for some hiking. There are several cafes and restrooms scattered around the Heath.

Victoria Park

Known for its boating lake, extensive playgrounds, and beautiful gardens. The park also hosts various events and festivals.

Practical Tips: Check the schedule for free concerts and events. The park has several cafes and picnic areas.

Walking Tours

Explore London on foot with these free and self-guided walking tours that let you discover the city's history, architecture, and culture.

South Bank Walk

Route: Start at the London Eye and walk along the Thames, passing landmarks like the Tate Modern, Shakespeare's Globe, and Tower Bridge.

Enjoy street performers, scenic views, and plenty of cafes and shops along the way.

Practical Tips: The walk is flat and accessible, making it suitable for strollers. Plan to stop at attractions along the route for breaks and refreshments.

Royal London Walk

Route: Begin at Buckingham Palace, then walk through St. James's Park to Westminster Abbey, the Houses of Parliament, and Big Ben.

Witness the Changing of the Guard at Buckingham Palace and enjoy the historical and political heart of London.

Practical Tips: Arrive early for the Changing of the Guard to secure a good spot. The walk is relatively short but packed with sights.

City of London Walk

Route: Start at St. Paul's Cathedral and explore the historic streets, including the Tower of London, Tower Bridge, and the Bank of England.

Discover the oldest part of London with its mix of ancient and modern architecture.

Practical Tips: Wear comfortable shoes and be prepared for some uneven surfaces and cobblestones. Many of the attractions have free entry days or hours.

Free Guided Walking Tours

Companies: Look for free walking tours offered by companies like Sandemans New Europe and Free Tours by Foot. These tours are tip-based, so while technically free, it's customary to tip the guide.

Knowledgeable guides provide fascinating insights into London's history and culture. Tours often cover different themes like Harry Potter, Jack the Ripper, or royal history.

Practical Tips: Check online for tour schedules and meeting points. Tours typically last 2-3 hours, so wear comfortable shoes and bring water.

Seasonal Events and Festivals

London hosts numerous free events and festivals throughout the year, offering a variety of cultural and entertainment experiences.

Notting Hill Carnival

When: August

Bank Holiday weekend Europe's largest street festival features vibrant parades, live music, and delicious Caribbean food.

Practical Tips: Arrive early to secure a good spot along the parade route. The event gets very crowded, so keep an eye on children and belongings.

Chinese New Year

When: January/February (dates vary)

Celebrate in Chinatown with dragon and lion dances, fireworks, and cultural performances.

Practical Tips: Check the schedule for parade times and plan to arrive early for a good view. Dress warmly, as the event takes place in winter.

Totally Thames Festival

When: September

A month-long celebration of the River Thames with free events including art installations, performances, and river races.

Practical Tips: Check the festival's website for a schedule of events and plan your visit around activities that interest your family.

London Marathon

When: April

Cheer on the runners along the route, which passes many of London's iconic landmarks.

Practical Tips: Find a spot along the route and bring snacks and drinks. The atmosphere is festive, and it's a great opportunity to see the city come alive.

Winter Wonderland

When: November to January

Held in Hyde Park, this festive event features rides, markets, ice skating, and live entertainment.

Practical Tips: Entry to the park is free, but attractions have fees. Visit during weekdays for smaller crowds and shorter lines.

Final Tips for Enjoying Free Activities in London

Plan Ahead: Research events and attractions before your visit to make the most of your time. Many places offer online resources and maps to help you plan.

Comfortable Clothing: Wear comfortable shoes and dress in layers to adapt to London's variable weather. Bring a small backpack for water, snacks, and any essentials.

Engage the Kids: Use activity trails and interactive exhibits to keep kids engaged and excited about what they're seeing and learning.

Stay Hydrated and Snack Smart: Carry water bottles and healthy snacks to keep everyone hydrated and energized, especially during walking tours and outdoor activities.

Check for Updates: Event schedules and opening hours can change, so check online for the latest information before heading out.

Enjoying London's free activities is a fantastic way to explore the city and create lasting memories without breaking the bank.

Shopping with Kids

London offers a diverse shopping experience that can be enjoyable for the whole family. From magical toy stores and charming bookshops to bustling markets and expansive malls, there's something to keep kids entertained and parents happy.

Here's a detailed guide to shopping with kids in London, including toy stores, bookshops, markets, malls, and the best places to find souvenirs and keepsakes.

Toy Stores and Bookshops

Hamleys

Location: Regent Street

Hamleys is one of the world's oldest and largest toy stores, spanning seven floors and filled with toys, games, and interactive experiences.

Practical Tips: Plan to spend at least a couple of hours here. The store can get very busy, so visit early in the day if possible.

The LEGO Store

Location: Leicester Square

The largest LEGO store in the world features impressive LEGO models, interactive building areas, and exclusive sets.

Personal Experience: The kids loved seeing the giant LEGO Big Ben and creating their own mini-figures. The interactive play areas kept them entertained for hours.

Practical Tips: The store can get crowded, especially on weekends. Consider visiting during off-peak hours for a more relaxed experience.

Waterstones Piccadilly

Location: Piccadilly Circus

The flagship Waterstones store has an extensive children's section with books, toys, and regular events like storytime and author readings.

Personal Experience: Our kids enjoyed browsing through the vast selection of books and participating in a storytelling session.

Practical Tips: Check the store's event schedule online and plan your visit around any interesting activities for children.

Foyles

Location: Charing Cross Road

This iconic bookstore has a dedicated children's section with a wide range of books, games, and regular events.

Practical Tips: Look out for special events and author visits, which can add an extra layer of excitement to your visit.

Markets and Malls

Covent Garden Market

Location: Covent Garden

This historic market is filled with unique shops, street performers, and food stalls. The Apple Market within Covent Garden features handmade crafts and souvenirs.

Practical Tips: The market can get busy, so visit early or during weekdays for a less crowded experience. Be sure to catch a street performance while you're there.

Camden Market

Location: Camden

Known for its eclectic mix of stalls, Camden Market offers everything from clothing and accessories to crafts and unique toys.

Practical Tips: The market is large and can be overwhelming, so plan your visit to specific sections. The food market is a great spot for lunch.

Westfield London

Location: White City

One of the largest shopping malls in Europe, Westfield London features a wide range of shops, restaurants, and entertainment options.

Personal Experience: The kids enjoyed visiting the large toy stores and the indoor play areas. We appreciated the convenience of having everything under one roof.

Practical Tips: Westfield can get very busy, especially on weekends. Plan to visit early in the day and take advantage of the family-friendly facilities like baby changing rooms and play areas.

Borough Market

Location: Southwark

While primarily a food market, Borough Market offers a variety of unique and artisanal products. It's a great place to find delicious treats and local products.

Practical Tips: Visit during the morning to avoid the lunchtime rush. Many stalls offer free samples, which can be a fun way to try new foods.

Souvenirs and Keepsakes

M&M's World

Location: Leicester Square

A four-story store dedicated to M&M's, offering personalized M&M's, themed merchandise, and interactive experiences.

Personal Experience: The kids were thrilled by the colorful displays and the chance to create their own custom M&M's.

Practical Tips: The store can get very crowded, so visit early or during off-peak hours. Allow time for the kids to explore and enjoy the interactive elements.

Harrods Toy Kingdom

Location: Knightsbridge

Harrods' Toy Kingdom is a wonderland of toys, games, and interactive displays. It's a great place to find high-quality and unique toys.

Practical Tips: Harrods can be overwhelming, so plan your visit to specific sections. The Toy Kingdom is on the third floor and is a must-visit.

Liberty London

Location: Regent Street

Known for its beautiful Tudor-style building and luxurious goods, Liberty London offers unique gifts and souvenirs, including children's toys and books.

Personal Experience: We enjoyed browsing the children's section, which features beautifully crafted toys and books.

Practical Tips: Liberty London is an upscale store, so be prepared for higher prices. It's a great place to find special keepsakes.

Fortnum & Mason

Location: Piccadilly

This historic department store is famous for its luxury food hampers, teas, and unique gifts. It's a great place to pick up traditional British souvenirs.

Personal Experience: We loved exploring the store's beautifully designed displays and picking out some delicious treats to take home.

Practical Tips: The store is especially charming during the holiday season, with festive decorations and gift options.

Final Tips for Shopping with Kids

Engage the Kids: Look for stores and markets that offer interactive experiences or demonstrations. This keeps the kids entertained and engaged.

Set a Budget: Discuss a budget with your children before heading out. This helps manage expectations and teaches them about making choices.

Take Breaks: Shopping can be tiring, so plan regular breaks for snacks and rest. Many shopping areas have cafes and rest areas.

Plan Ahead: Research the stores and markets you want to visit and plan your route. This helps make the most of your time and ensures you don't miss any must-see spots.

Safety First: Keep an eye on your children, especially in busy markets and stores. Establish a meeting point in case you get separated.

Shopping in London can be a fun and memorable experience for the whole family. With these tips and recommendations, you're sure to find the best spots for toys, books, souvenirs, and more. Enjoy your shopping adventure in London!

Cultural Tips and Etiquette

Understanding and respecting cultural norms and etiquette can greatly enhance your experience when visiting London.

Understanding British Manners

Politeness and Courtesy

Personal Experience: British people are known for their politeness and courtesy. Simple acts of kindness, like holding the door open or saying "please" and "thank you," go a long way.

Practical Tips: Always greet people with a friendly "hello" or "good morning." Use "please" when making requests and "thank you" to show appreciation.

Queuing (Standing in Line)

Personal Experience: Queuing is a fundamental part of British culture. People expect everyone to wait their turn patiently.

Practical Tips: Always join the back of the queue and wait your turn. Cutting in line is considered very rude. If you're unsure where the queue starts, politely ask.

Greetings and Introductions

Personal Experience: Handshakes are the most common form of greeting in a formal or business setting. In more casual settings, a simple "hi" or "hello" is sufficient.

Practical Tips: When meeting someone for the first time, offer a handshake and introduce yourself. Address people by their title and last name until invited to use their first name.

Conversation

Personal Experience: British people often engage in small talk about the weather, travel, or general topics before moving on to more serious subjects.

Practical Tips: Avoid controversial topics like politics or personal finances in casual conversation. Complimenting someone's home, garden, or a meal they've prepared is always appreciated.

Tipping

Personal Experience: Tipping is common in restaurants, taxis, and for personal services like haircuts. However, it's not as obligatory as in some other countries.

Practical Tips: In restaurants, a tip of 10-15% is standard if service isn't included in the bill. Tipping in bars is not expected, but you can round up the bill. For taxis, rounding up to the nearest pound is customary.

Navigating Cultural Differences

Public Transport Etiquette

Personal Experience: London's public transport system is extensive and widely used. It's important to follow certain etiquette to ensure a smooth journey.

Practical Tips: Allow passengers to exit before you board the train or bus. Keep to the right on escalators to allow people to pass on the left. Avoid talking loudly and keep phone conversations to a minimum.

Punctuality

Personal Experience: Punctuality is valued in British culture, both for social and business appointments.

Practical Tips: Always aim to arrive on time. If you're running late, it's courteous to inform the person you're meeting as soon as possible.

Personal Space and Privacy

Personal Experience: British people value their personal space and privacy. It's considered polite to keep a reasonable distance when conversing and to avoid intrusive questions.

Practical Tips: Respect personal space, especially in crowded places. Avoid asking overly personal questions, especially when you first meet someone.

Dress Code

Personal Experience: Dress codes can vary depending on the setting. London is generally quite casual, but it's good to dress smartly for certain occasions.

Practical Tips: For dining out or attending the theater, smart casual attire is usually appropriate. In business settings, a suit and tie or equivalent business attire is standard.

Humor

Personal Experience: British humor is often subtle, self-deprecating, and may include irony and understatement.

Practical Tips: Don't be surprised if someone jokes about themselves or a situation in a way that seems understated. Joining in with light-hearted banter is usually welcomed.

Tips for a Smooth Stay

Accommodation

London offers a wide range of accommodation options, from hotels and hostels to vacation rentals and serviced apartments.

Practical Tips: Book accommodation well in advance, especially during peak tourist seasons. Research the area to ensure it's close to public transport and amenities.

Money and Payments

Credit and debit cards are widely accepted, but it's always good to have some cash on hand for small purchases or markets.

Practical Tips: Notify your bank of your travel plans to avoid issues with your cards. ATMs are widely available, and contactless payment is common.

Safety

London is generally safe, but like any major city, it's important to stay aware of your surroundings.

Practical Tips: Keep your belongings secure, especially in crowded areas. Avoid walking alone late at night in unfamiliar areas. Use reputable taxi services or public transport.

Language

English is the primary language spoken, but London's diverse population means you'll hear many languages.

Practical Tips: If English isn't your first language, most Londoners will appreciate your effort to speak it. Carry a phrasebook or translation app if needed.

Healthcare

London has excellent healthcare facilities, with both private and public (NHS) options available.

Practical Tips: Travel insurance is essential to cover any medical expenses. If you need medical assistance, pharmacies are a good first point of contact for minor issues.

Technology and Connectivity

Wi-Fi is widely available in hotels, cafes, and public places. Mobile networks are reliable and offer good coverage.

Practical Tips: Consider getting a local SIM card if you plan to use your phone frequently. Many cafes and public spaces offer free Wi-Fi, but it's good to have a backup plan for connectivity.

Dining Out

Personal Experience: London's dining scene is incredibly diverse, offering cuisine from all over the world.

Practical Tips: Make reservations for popular restaurants, especially on weekends. Many places offer online booking. Don't be afraid to ask for recommendations from locals or hotel staff.

Public Restrooms

Public restrooms can be found in major tourist areas, parks, and department stores. Many require a small fee.

Practical Tips: Carry some change for restroom fees. Use facilities in cafes or museums if needed.

Weather Preparedness

London's weather can be unpredictable, with rain possible at any time of year.

Practical Tips: Always carry an umbrella and wear layers. Check the weather forecast daily to plan your attire.

By understanding and respecting British manners and cultural norms, navigating London becomes much easier and more enjoyable. With these tips and practical advice, you're well-equipped to have a smooth and memorable stay in this vibrant and dynamic city.

Health and Safety

Ensuring the health and safety of your family during your visit to London is crucial for a smooth and enjoyable trip. Here's a detailed guide on the nearest hospitals and clinics, emergency numbers, and child safety tips.

Nearest Hospitals and Clinics

Hospitals

St Thomas' Hospital

Location: Westminster Bridge Road, SE1 7EH

Services: A major NHS teaching hospital with a 24-hour Accident & Emergency (A&E) department.

University College Hospital

Location: 235 Euston Road, NW1 2BU

Services: Another major NHS teaching hospital with a comprehensive range of services and a 24-hour A&E department.

Personal Experience: Modern facilities and a strong reputation for excellent medical care.

The Royal London Hospital

Location: Whitechapel Road, E1 1BB

Services: Part of Barts Health NHS Trust, it offers a wide range of specialist services and a 24-hour A&E department.

Known for its expertise and comprehensive emergency care.

Clinics

NHS Walk-In Centres

General Information: These clinics offer treatment for minor injuries and illnesses without needing an appointment.

Notable Locations

The Soho NHS Walk-in Centre: 1 Frith Street, W1D 3HZ

Victoria NHS Walk-in Centre: 63 Buckingham Gate, SW1E 6AT

Private Clinics

The London Clinic

Location: 20 Devonshire Place, W1G 6BW

Services: A leading private hospital offering a range of medical services and consultations.

Harley Street Clinics

General Information: Harley Street in Marylebone is renowned for its numerous private clinics and specialists.

Practical Tips

Health Insurance: Ensure you have travel insurance that covers medical expenses. Some private clinics may require upfront payment.

Pharmacies: Pharmacies, known as chemists in the UK, can provide advice and over-the-counter medications for minor health issues. Boots and Superdrug are two major pharmacy chains with locations throughout London.

Emergency Numbers

Emergency Services (Police, Fire, Ambulance): 999

Use: For any life-threatening emergencies or if you need immediate assistance from the police, fire brigade, or medical services.

Operators are trained to handle emergencies efficiently. Clearly state your location and the nature of the emergency.

Non-Emergency Medical Assistance (NHS Direct): 111

Use: For non-emergency medical advice or if you're unsure whether you need to go to the hospital. NHS 111 can provide guidance and direct you to the appropriate services.

Personal Experience: Useful for medical concerns that don't require immediate emergency care. The service is available 24/7.

Non-Emergency Police Assistance: 101

Use: For non-urgent matters that require police attention, such as reporting a crime that has already happened or seeking advice.
Ideal for situations where immediate emergency response is not needed but police involvement is required.

Practical Tips

Save Numbers: Program these emergency numbers into your phone for quick access.

Know Your Location: Always be aware of your current location, including the nearest landmarks, to provide accurate information in case of an emergency.

Child Safety Tips

General Safety

Supervision: Always supervise young children closely, especially in crowded areas and tourist attractions.

Identification: Equip your child with identification, such as a wristband with your contact information, in case you get separated.

Meeting Points: Establish a meeting point in case you get separated. Make sure your child knows where to go and who to approach for help.

Transport Safety

Public Transport: Teach your child to stay close to you and hold hands while using public transport. Explain the importance of staying behind the yellow line on platforms.

Car Seats: If you're renting a car, ensure you have the appropriate car seat for your child's age and size. Many rental companies offer car seats for hire.

Health and Hygiene

Hand Washing: Encourage frequent hand washing, especially before meals and after using the restroom. Carry hand sanitizer for situations where soap and water aren't available.

First Aid Kit: Pack a basic first aid kit with essentials like band-aids, antiseptic wipes, and any necessary medications.

Outdoor Safety

Sun Protection: Use sunscreen, hats, and sunglasses to protect your child from the sun. Even on cloudy days, UV rays can be harmful.

Water Safety: Supervise your child closely near water bodies, such as pools, fountains, or the Thames River. Teach them about water safety rules.

Stranger Danger

Awareness: Teach your child to be cautious of strangers and to never go anywhere with someone they don't know. Explain the importance of finding a uniformed staff member or police officer if they need help.

Code Word: Establish a family code word that only you and your child know. They can use this word if someone claims to know you and offers to take them somewhere.

Technology and Communication

Mobile Phones: If your child is old enough, provide them with a mobile phone and teach them how to use it to contact you in an emergency.

Contact Information: Make sure your child knows your phone number and the name and address of your accommodation.

Cultural Awareness

Local Customs: Teach your child about local customs and etiquette to ensure they understand how to behave appropriately in different situations.

Respect for Rules: Emphasize the importance of following rules, whether it's staying on the pavement, obeying traffic signals, or being quiet in museums.

By understanding the local health and safety resources, knowing the emergency numbers, and following these child safety tips, you can ensure a safer and more enjoyable visit to London for your family. Stay prepared and stay safe!

Tips for an Unforgettable Trip

Planning a trip to London can be exciting but also a bit overwhelming given the vast array of things to see and do. Here are some tips to help you create an itinerary, keep kids entertained, and make the most of your visit for an unforgettable experience.

Creating an Itinerary

Research and Prioritize

Start by listing the top attractions and experiences you don't want to miss. Consider the interests of all family members when planning.

Practical Tips: Use travel guides, websites, and apps like TripAdvisor or Visit London to identify key attractions. Create a wish list and prioritize them based on your interests and time available.

Plan by Location

Personal Experience: Group attractions by their locations to minimize travel time and make the most of each day.

Practical Tips: Divide your itinerary into sections (e.g., central London, west London) and plan to visit nearby attractions on the same day. For example, you can visit Buckingham Palace, St. James's Park, and Westminster Abbey in one day since they are close to each other.

Include Downtime

Personal Experience: Make sure to include downtime in your itinerary to rest and recharge, especially if traveling with kids.

Practical Tips: Plan for breaks in parks, cafes, or at your accommodation. Allocate time for leisurely activities like picnics or strolls through markets.

Mix Popular and Hidden Gems

Personal Experience: Combining major attractions with lesser-known spots can give you a more rounded experience of London.

Practical Tips: Include popular sights like the Tower of London and the British Museum, but also explore local markets, hidden gardens, and unique neighborhoods like Notting Hill or Shoreditch.

Flexible Scheduling

Personal Experience: Keep your schedule flexible to allow for spontaneous activities and unexpected discoveries.

Practical Tips: Plan must-see activities but leave gaps in your itinerary for impromptu exploration. Check the weather forecast daily and adjust your plans accordingly.

Keeping Kids Entertained

Interactive Museums and Attractions

Kids often enjoy hands-on and interactive experiences more than passive sightseeing.

Practical Tips: Visit museums like the Science Museum and the Natural History Museum, which offer interactive exhibits. The London Transport Museum and the Harry Potter Studio Tour are also great for engaging children.

Parks and Playgrounds

London's parks offer a great way for kids to burn off energy and enjoy the outdoors.

Practical Tips: Spend time in parks like Hyde Park, Regent's Park, and Greenwich Park. Look for playgrounds like the Diana Memorial Playground or the Princess Diana Memorial Fountain for water play on hot days.

Themed Activities

Themed activities and tours can make sightseeing more exciting for kids.

Practical Tips: Consider a Harry Potter walking tour, a treasure hunt, or a boat ride on the Thames. KidZania in Westfield London offers a unique role-playing experience for children.

Local Treats

Sampling local treats can be a fun and tasty way to keep kids happy.

Practical Tips: Visit bakeries and cafes like Ben's Cookies, Gail's Bakery, or Fortnum & Mason for afternoon tea. The M&M's World and the LEGO Store also offer sweet treats and fun experiences.

Public Transport Adventures

Using London's public transport can be an adventure in itself for kids.

Practical Tips: Ride the top deck of a double-decker bus, take a boat trip on the Thames, or experience the London Underground. The Emirates Air Line cable car offers stunning views and a unique ride.

Making the Most of Your Visit

Advance Bookings

Booking tickets in advance can save time and money.

Practical Tips: Purchase tickets for major attractions, shows, and tours online before your trip. Look for family discounts and package deals.

Early Starts and Late Visits

Starting early or visiting attractions late can help you avoid the busiest times.

Practical Tips: Arrive at popular attractions like the Tower of London or the London Eye when they open or visit them later in the day. This can reduce wait times and crowds.

Local Insights

Local insights can enhance your experience and lead to discovering hidden gems.

Practical Tips: Chat with locals, hotel staff, or tour guides for recommendations on restaurants, activities, and lesser-known sights. Consider joining free walking tours for insider knowledge.

Use Travel Passes

Travel passes can save money and make getting around easier.

Practical Tips: Consider getting an Oyster card or a contactless payment card for public transport. Tourist passes like the London Pass offer entry to multiple attractions and can be cost-effective.

Stay Connected

Personal Experience: Staying connected with mobile data or Wi-Fi can help with navigation and planning on the go.

Practical Tips: Purchase a local SIM card or an international data plan. Many cafes, museums, and public spaces offer free Wi-Fi.

Capture the Memories

Documenting your trip helps preserve the memories.

Practical Tips: Take plenty of photos and videos, but also take moments to enjoy experiences without the camera. Encourage kids to keep a travel journal or create a scrapbook.

Pack Essentials

Packing the right essentials can make your day trips smoother.

Practical Tips: Bring a daypack with water bottles, snacks, a map, hand sanitizer, and a small first aid kit.

Dress in layers and carry an umbrella for London's unpredictable weather.

Respect Local Customs

Personal Experience: Respecting local customs and etiquette ensures a pleasant experience.

Practical Tips: Follow local norms regarding queuing, politeness, and tipping. Be mindful of your surroundings and the people around you.

By following these tips and creating a well-balanced itinerary, you can ensure an unforgettable trip to London that caters to everyone in the family.

Useful Resources

Having the right resources at your fingertips can significantly enhance your experience in London. Here are some essential apps, websites, and online guides to help you navigate the city, find attractions, and make the most of your visit.

Apps for Navigating London

Citymapper

Citymapper is an all-in-one transit app that helps you navigate London's public transport system, including buses, trains, and the Underground.

Features: Real-time updates, multiple route options, step-by-step directions, and integration with ride-sharing services.

This app is a lifesaver for getting around London efficiently. It's user-friendly and provides accurate information.

Download: Available on iOS and Android.

Transport for London (TfL) Oyster and Contactless

The official TfL app allows you to manage your Oyster card, check your balance, and top up on the go.

Features: Real-time service updates, fare information, journey planning, and access to contactless payment history.

It's convenient for managing travel expenses and staying updated on service disruptions.

Download: Available on iOS and Android.

Google Maps

Google Maps is a versatile navigation app that provides directions for driving, walking, cycling, and public transport.

Features: Real-time traffic updates, offline maps, restaurant and attraction reviews, and detailed route information.

Reliable for finding routes and nearby attractions. The offline maps feature is handy for areas with poor connectivity.

Download: Available on iOS and Android.

Visit London Official City Guide

The official app from Visit London provides comprehensive information on attractions, events, and itineraries.

Features: Personalized recommendations, offline maps, event listings, and deals on tickets and experiences.

Great for discovering new events and getting the latest tourism updates.

Download: Available on iOS and Android.

Uber

Uber is a popular ride-sharing app that allows you to book private rides across London.

Features: Real-time tracking, fare estimates, various ride options, and cashless payments.

Useful for quick and reliable transport, especially late at night or when public transport is limited.

Download: Available on iOS and Android.

Free Now (formerly mytaxi)

Free Now is a taxi-hailing app that connects you with licensed black cabs and private hire vehicles in London.

Features: Real-time tracking, fare estimates, multiple payment options, and the ability to book rides in advance.

Convenient for hailing traditional black cabs and ensuring safe, reliable rides.

Download: Available on iOS and Android.

Time Out London

The Time Out London app offers recommendations for events, restaurants, bars, and attractions.

Features: Event listings, reviews, venue information, and personalized recommendations.

Excellent for finding out what's happening in the city and getting insider tips.

Download: Available on iOS and Android.

Maps

SCAN QR CODE
TO VIEW MAPS

Made in the USA
Middletown, DE
03 November 2024